Charlie Adams has written comedy material for some of the UK's funniest comedians including Mike Yarwood and for Bob Hope's British performances. He has written sketches and gags for major BBC radio programmes including *Don't stop now – it's fundation*, and has just completed his eighth series of the award-winning *The News Huddlines*. He is currently writing a series of situation comedy for Roy Kinnear and Andrew Sachs called *Sloecoaches*. Charlie Adams was born in Glasgow and apart from a year in New York in 1976 has lived in Kent for the last seventeen years.

Gareth Hale was born in London and now resides in the swish pastures of Woolwich, south-east London. Gareth is interested in theatre, people and this crazy thing we call life. His ambition is to do something useful in the world or to be interviewed on the *Miss World* tv programme.

Norman Pace was brought up in the market town of Newark, Nottinghamshire where he was educated at the Magnus Grammar School. In 1971, at the age of eighteen, Norman moved to south-east London to attend Avery Hill College of Education during which time he began writing and performing comedy with Gareth Hale. Norman is a member of the Fundation comedy team who have been packing them in at the Tramshed Theatre, Woolwich, south London for some seven years and are at present busy putting together the third series of their sucessful Radio 4 comedy show – *Don't stop now – it's fundation*. As Hale and Pace Norman and Gareth have appeared many times on television. Some credits include *Pushing up daisies*, *The tube*, *The Jim Davidson show*, *The laughter show*, *The Lenny Henry show* and *The young ones*.

Steve Lockett was born in Deptford and now lives in Greenwich, south-east London. He studied at Avery Hill College and went to San Francisco to play professional soccer for the Golden Gate Gaels. He has worked on sports illustrations and children's books and has been exhibiting around London . . . his case comes up next week.

Dedication

With special thanks to Alan Nixon of the BBC
without whom this book would still have been
possible.

Falsies

forged diaries of the famous

Charlie Adams, Gareth Hale and Norman Pace

Cartoons and illustrations by Steve Lockett

Robson Books

First published in the United Kingdom in 1985 by
Robson Books Ltd, Bolsover House, 5–6 Clipstone Street,
London W1P 7EB.

British Library Cataloguing in Publication Data
  Adams, Charles
    Falsies: forged diaries of the famous.
    I. Title II. Hale, Gareth   III. Pace, Norman
    828′.91409   PN6175

  ISBN 0-86051-351-3

Typeset by Spire Print Services Ltd, Salisbury, Wilts
Printed in the United Kingdom by St Edmundsbury Press, Bury
St Edmunds, Suffolk.

Contents

NEIL ARMSTRONG

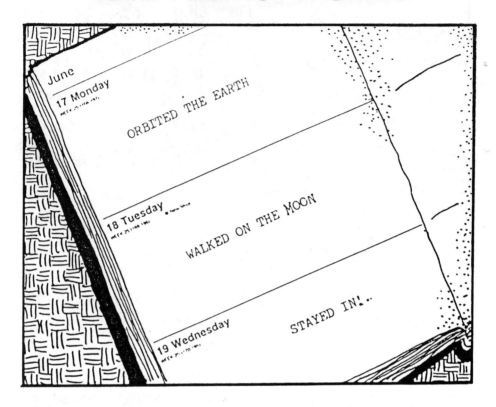

ARCHIMEDES

HANS CHRISTIAN ANDERSEN

Tuesday	—Still living happily every after.
Wednesday	—Ditto
Thursday	—Ditto.
Friday	—Ditto.
Saturday	—Ditto.
Sunday	—Ditto.
Monday	—Ditto.

FRED ASTAIRE

28 Wednesday

WEEK 35 (240 125)

Rogered Ginger!

MUHAMMED ALI

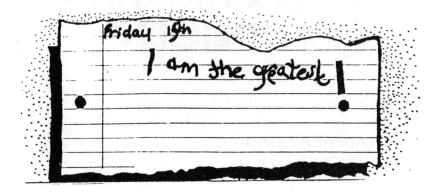

ATLAS

WOODY ALLEN

Hi diary—Jeez, what a day. I'm still no further with my latest film script, 'Everything You Wanted to Know About Paranoia But Didn't Dare Ask'. God, I'm such a failure, I wish I was dead. But then again you know, being dead is just like being alive but without the breathing part. At least if I was dead I could look forward to a more successful sex life. A casual affair with a passing worm, I don't know. My life is like a one-way lift, forever going down.

Talking of which, my girlfriend Rebecca came over for dinner tonight. She's understanding, sensitive and sincere and besides, she's got great tits. When she arrived I did the usual things, like poured a couple of drinks down her dress, got really tongue-tied, fumbled to light her cigarette and set her hair on fire, then made a grab at her and missed coz I'd taken my glasses off so I wouldn't look such a myopic, sexually hung-up, underfed, balding, neurotic Jewish jerk. I put on some music to kinda ease the situation, Vivaldi's Four Seasons. I guess Vivaldi must have taken over when Frankie Valli left.

Over dinner we spoke only in sub-titles, I think it's best to say what you mean. She refused to eat her scrambled eggs, and she was put off by the thought of battered unborn chickens. What a time to get maternal. Anyone would think I'd asked her to eat a pork chop—wrapped in ham. Rebecca said I was the most amazing person she'd ever met. In all her years as a psychiatrist, I was the first man she'd ever met who suffered from penis envy. That's what you get from dating your analyst.

ATTILA

ACHILLES

KING ARTHUR

This morning I awoke to great pain. Within my skull raged a fury such as I have never felt before. I summoned Merlin to my side and commanded him to prepare a balm for this agony within my head. Ere long he brought an elixir that he promised would solve my plight made from a magic mushroom that grows in the mystical forest.

I shall take it straightway!

• • • • • • • • • • • • •

Hey man, this potion's some real heavy shit! This Merlin's pushing some far-out gear. Like I was on a downer last week so Merlin gave me a special potion to take. It really blew my mind, I was by the lake, right, strumming . . . .

"..... 'where have all the flowers gone' on my lute, when I see this sword in a stone. Hey — a sword getting stoned! It's called Excalibur; sounds like some new sort of LSD. I believe in love not war, so I threw the sword in the lake.

Then hey, hang on to your Jesus sandals, this synchronised swimmer chick goes past and catches it and sinks below the surface, heavy metal! So you know like, my mind is blown, so I go back to my pad to grab a few Z's. Then I hear this weird clanking sound coming from Guinevere's chamber, like Hawkwind being played backwards. So I go to her room and she's pulling this gigantic pink salmon out of the biggest tin can I've ever seen. Then I realise it's Lancelot in his armour getting his rocks off! Some salmon — So that's why they call him Lancelot!!"

B ALEXANDER GRAHAM BELL

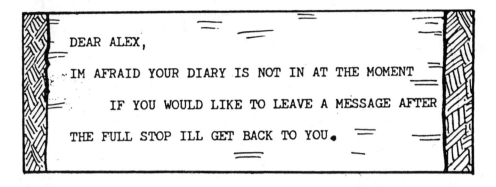

DEAR ALEX,

IM AFRAID YOUR DIARY IS NOT IN AT THE MOMENT

IF YOU WOULD LIKE TO LEAVE A MESSAGE AFTER

THE FULL STOP ILL GET BACK TO YOU.

LORD BYRON

January 17th 1818

Had Lamb for lunch. Had her husband for afters. And it's nice to hear they've named a ball-point pen after me.

ROGER BANNISTER

May 6th 1954

Gone out for a run. Be back in about four minutes.

ZOLA BUDD

August 1984

Dear Diary,

Today I bumped into someone I've always admired. . .

BATMAN

DEAR DIARY...
....

10 AM AND COMMISSIONER GORDON CALLS ON THE BATPHONE........

BRRING!

HE HAS IN URGENT NEED OF BATMAN AND ROBIN, UPKEEPERS OF LAW AND ORDER AND ALL ROUND GOOD GUYS........

...PENGUIN WAS AT THAT VERY MOMENT STEALING A ZILLION DOLLAR HAUL OF DIAMONDS!

TO THE BATPOLE!

10.05 SLID DOWN BATPOLE

YIPE! ...

MUST GET ALFRED TO GREASE THE BATPOLE MORE OFTEN —— IVE LADDERED 3 PAIRS OF TIGHTS ALREADY THIS WEEK!

HOLY TRANSVESTITE! — I THINK WE'VE COME DOWN THE WRONG BATPOLE

CONTINUED TO GOTHAM CITY..

... TO PUT PAID TO PENGUIN'S PERVERTED PRANKISH PLAN. ARRIVED IN NICK OF TIME BEFORE THE FOUL FOWL AND HIS CLUCKING ARMY HAD TIME TO FLY THE COOP. NORMALLY I ABHOR VIOLENCE BUT TO MAKE AMERICA A BETTER PLACE TO LIVE IN I WAS FORCED TO USE A REASONABLE AMOUNT OF FORCE ......

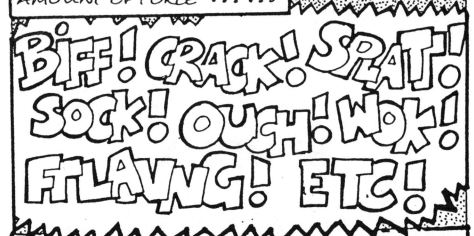

BIFF! CRACK! SPLAT! SOCK! OUCH! WOK! FTLAVNG! ETC!

PENGUIN'S WINGS ARE CLIPPED. NO MORE FELONIOUS FLIGHTS OF FANCY FOR THIS JAILBIRD WHO WILL REMAIN PERMANENTLY PENNED IN THE PENAL PENITENTIARY.

STOPPED OFF ON THE WAY HOME TO BUY SOME MORE OF THOSE NICE BLACK SATIN UNDER PANTS ....

.... THOUGHT ABOUT DOING SOME GOOD DEEDS THEN HAD AN EARLY NIGHT!

ZZZZZZZ

BEETHOVEN

April 9th 1795

Finished my ninth today. Told number ten she'll have to wait till tomorrow.

BUDDHA

'Silicone injection seems to have taken.'

HUMPHREY BOGART

November 4th

Damn women drivers. Of all the cars in all the world she had to reverse into mine.

BUNSEN

THURS. 15th

INVENTED THE BUNSEN BURNER

— WORKING ON ASBESTOS WHEN HAND HEALS!

BADEN-POWELL

September 3rd

Discovered Boy Scout movement. Put it in a bucket. Wrote new camp-fire song. It goes: Ging gang goolie goolie goolie goolie watch'er . . . inspiration came to me after I hurdled the barbed wire fence. My new organisation will help the youth of our great British Empire to take life seriously . . . dib dib dib dob dob dob.

'If you rub a little harder we'll both get warmed up.'

BISMARCK

October 11th 1902

Went out with the lads and sank a few.

SITTING BULL

Sunday

Many men came today, with long knives. They killed um heap lot of Buffalo and ate um all meat we were saving for winter. That's the last time I have um Squaw's family to dinner.

Squaw tried to make up by giving me new delicacy.

'What um this?' I asked.

'Buffalo pancakes,' she replied.

'Delicious,' I said. 'Did you make um?'

'No, the buffalo did.'

Saw that bluecoat Custer today . . . we call him Yellowhair. That'll teach him to carry his baby on his head.

Monday

Tonight is the night of the many moons—squaws' bath night.

I feel in um bones that soon I must go to meet my father in the Happy Hunting Grounds. He's keeping my place in the queue outside Hiawatha's Massage Parlour. Must dash.

RONALD BIGGS

RABBIE BURNS

March 22nd

Wrote new poem today.

> Wee beastie creepie nae sae crae,
> Wi' muckle kiltie krankie bairn.
> Yon bonnie lassie tak the glen,
> Tae wee jock's maether's kin the burn.
> Hoots Mon Tammie gang awa'
> A braw brae nicht the cannie kirk.
> Tae gae galumphin och just noo
> A coerin' slashie frae yon dirk.

Nae idea what it means, but the tourists love it.

ENID BLYTON

Monday

What a glorious day! The sun was sparkling high in a clear blue English sky like a giant yellow balloon on the first day of the hols. I took Timmy for a jolly exciting morning walk across the moors, during which we jolly well bumped into a couple of jolly interesting millionaires in the process of being kidnapped by several rather suspicious characters with swarthy skins, shifty eyes and exaggerated European accents. Timmy started snapping at their ankles which was somewhat embarrassing since he's my husband.

By the time we returned to Rose Cottage we were jolly ravenous and soon tucked into heaps of steak and kidney pudding followed by dozens of freshly-baked blackberry tarts with lashings of cream all washed down by home-made dandelion and burdock. It was jolly good fun raiding the larder at Rose Cottage but unfortunately the owners turned up and threatened to report us to the police so we rushed back home in time for a yummy tea-time feast in our specially built mock-up of a public school dorm with Ginger, Fatty, Peta and a few more of our OAP friends. Bed at 10 pm. Up with Timmy for a midnight feast. The jolly old earth moved. Yum yum.

Tuesday

What a glorious day, the sun was sparkling high in a clear blue English sky like a giant yellow balloon on the first day . . .

Wednesday

What a glorious day, the sun was sparkling high in a clear blue English sky like a giant yellow balloon . . .

Thursday

What a glorious day, the sun was sparkling high in a clear blue English sky . . .

Friday

What a glorious day . . .

Saturday

Glorious . . .

Sunday

What?

MARLON BRANDO

C RAYMOND CHANDLER

Monday

It was a day like any other day, 24 hours long and ending in a 'y'.
As I lurched towards the coffee pot the cold linoleum told my feet
it was 7.30 am. My feet tried to tell my brain, but my brain was
playing hard to get. It was singing a song all of its own. A crazy,
wild kind of song that was all too familiar. A song about a dame
and an empty bottle of bourbon. I felt a wave of nausea wash over
me. What was happening? My feet were telling the time, my brain
was singing a song and now my stomach was out to lunch. Yes, life
is hard, but then again so's a 2,000 piece jigsaw, and somehow I
had to fit the pieces together.

It had been a night like any other night. A lonely bar in a lonely
town. A bottle of bourbon my only friend, inviting me for a drink

that then made casual conversation with my gut. The way she burst into the room she could have been an inflatable. She had more curves than a plateful of spaghetti, and with a figure like that she could get arrested just for breathing in. Her conversation was stunning. She really had a way with monosyllables. Built she was, smart she was not. If she'd had as much up-top as she had up-top, she would have had to wear a D cup brassiere on her head. She thought Jean-Paul Sartre was a brand of cigarettes and Fellini was just a high class name for oral sex. The only culture she had was growing between her toes. Of course, I immediately fell in love with her. OK, she was no Einstein, and there again $E = mc^2$ whatever that means.

She'd been around. She'd done more tricks than Paul Daniels and thought that trousers were just an accessory before the fact. I knew it could never work between us, it was like climbing Everest in a pair of roller skates—I was going nowhere fast. She left, what a dame. Huh, Dame is just an anagram of MADE, which is another anagram of EDAM—hard cheese. Romance is like throwing up over the side of the New Jersey ferry in a gale. At first you feel good but then it always comes back in your face.

It was time I wised up—but the only wisdom I had I used to brush my teeth. Yeah, she was a dame like any other dame, farewell my lovely. Heh, that seemed like a good title for a book. I slumped down in front of the typewriter, and tapped out the first sentence. 'It was a day like any other day'.

PRINCE CHARMING

Saturday

Got so absolutely blotto on the good old hooch last night that I abs'lutely can't jolly well remember who the two debs were that I was out with. Probably a couple of gels I picked up at the Gymkhana. Sissie's friends I shouldn't wonder. Mummy's insisting I attend some state function or other this afto. But with a bit of luck I'll be able to sneak off and lock myself in the Throne Room with one of the old man's girlie mags.

Sunday

Disaster, Mummy's furious. Jolly well woke up to find oneself splattered all over the Sunday gutter-press. Talk about infringement of personal liberties. It's a bit much when a prince can't give some bird a good time in a public place without some grubby little pleb with a camera snapping off a quick 8″ by 10″. Don't recognise the girl but rather a good profile of one's truly, jolly handsome, what?

Monday

Big brother rang up to have a man-to-man with me. Droned on and on about discretion and keeping up appearances.

Tuesday

Boring day. Nothing about me in the papers.

Wednesday

Another disgusting piece of gutter journalism in one of the smutty Fleet Street rags today. It really isn't fair printing the truth about us Royals. After all, one can't fight back you know. Mummy says if I don't toe the jolly old line she is going to cut my allowance. How am I going to survive on only six actresses a week?

Thursday

Bored.

Friday

I'm in trouble with the newspapers again—they won't let me forget I 'accidentally' sprayed some of them with paint. One couldn't help it, one was bored. That's not what upset them—it was when I went back to sand them down for a second coat.

WILLIAM CAXTON

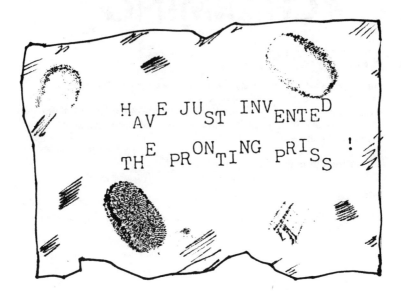

H_AVE JUST INVENTED
TH^E PR_ON_TI^NG PRI_S_S !

WINSTON CHURCHILL

December 6th . . .

Never in the field of human conflict have so few given so much to so many . . . ah well, that's AIDS for you.

DAVY CROCKETT

June 22nd . . .

Went to the doctor. Got this funny thing growing out of the back of my neck.

KING CANUTE

February 15th . . .

Wife's waters broke today. Did my best.

DR CRIPPEN

Haven't seen the wife for some time.

CUSTER

Surrounded by Indians . . . just when I fancied a Chinese.

COPERNICUS

Discovered that the Sun is the centre of the Universe. Rupert Murdoch is delighted.

CALIGULA

Monday XXVI Janus

Another orgy today. What a yawn. Went to bed with three legionnaires and a large goat. The legionnaires were husky but unimaginative. Having arrived in full battle-dress they said they didn't know where to put their spears. The goat had no such inhibitions. The goat's called Billyus Maximus 'cos he farts a lot. That legionnaire's got my goat.

Tuesday

Lazy day. Got up at X o'clock. Then again at XI o'clock, again at XII o'clock and twice in the afternoon. That goat's insatiable. Caught legionnaire's disease.

Wednesday

Just learned that today is named after the Norse god Woden. Invited him round. What a disappointment. He calls himself a god but he doesn't even know what paedophilia means and he has the sexual technique of an insurance man. Still, I did manage to persuade him to come to my 'stark raving mad' classes. Thor's day tomorrow. Ugh. Thank god for the goat.

Thursday

Thor came round. Had him. Poisoned him. The goat got haemor-
rhoids and decided to audition for 'The Romans in Britain'. He
says it's an allegory but I think it's an infection of the anus.

Friday

Went to Desiderata's Perverted Sex for the Under 12s party. Very
boring. All the under 12s are a bunch of washed-out old pros,
there's no freshness any more. The under 5s are exactly the same,
I wonder if it's possible to have it away with an unborn foetus. I
must ask mother.

Had giant row with the goat today. He says I treat him as a sex
object without any regard for him as a real person. I told him that
this was not true, that I loved him. Then I slit his throat and ate
him for lunch. A screw and a meal in one small body.

What a tiring week. Thank god it's the weekend. Looking forward to putting my feet up. Mmm, now why didn't I think of that
before I ate the goat?

Saturday

Slept with mother. Poisoned father. Watched Benny Hill Show.
It's disgusting.

LADY CHATTERLEY

Mellors and I had a slight mishap today. He was applying the sexual lubricant and he got his head stuck in the bucket.

He has been a thorn in my side, ever since I made him that floral chain for . . for . . . him. Next time I won't use roses.

Husband suspects, I'm sure. Today he asked to see the *old* MOT for his wheelchair.

Mellors is insatiable. Today as I pushed my husband in his wheelchair, Mellors made love to me. My husband said nothing; I found it pleasant but the rest of the queue complained.

Weird chap with a beard following us, writing in a tattered notebook. Hope he's not from the Sun.

CEZANNE

March 23rd . . .
Paul Gauguin told me today I was the father of modern art.

'It's an abstract, Mr Cézanne!'

ROBINSON CRUSOE

CAIN

BC. 23000000½

Killed my brother today. Not a lot of people know that. Wish I hadn't. It's his turn to do the dishes.

CINDERELLA

December 26 . . .

Buttons came off on my dress again. I wish he'd stop wearing it. I was busy in the kitchen, painting the coal and thinking about the ball at the Palace tonight and how I couldn't go because I hadn't been invited and didn't have a dress anyway when suddenly there was a blinding flash . . . and I thought I'd left the lid off the Ajax foaming cleanser in the bog again . . . but when I looked there was a little old lady who said I could go to the ball because she had a dress for me. She said she had a magic wand and I said I've heard that before, but she said no, she wasn't like the others in the play . . . men dressed up. She said she could make me a coach out of a pumpkin and I said, oh what a pity you didn't tell me that yesterday, we just ate the last pumpkin. Stupid bag. What the hell's a pumpkin? So she made it out of a jaffa instead. Anyway, pretty soon I'm off to the ball in a lovely gown, a coach with horses and four coachmen. I danced all night with Prince Charming and I told him I had to be home by midnight and he said that was a shame because he wanted me to go up and see his quarters. I said I could already feel them quite nicely through his tights. Then the clock struck twelve and as I started to rush home before all my things turned back into rags I only went and lost one of my glass slippers. Anyway, diary, the next day Prince Charming comes round proclaiming that he's found this slipper and whoever it fits he will wed. Well, he was delighted when it fitted and I hope he'll be very happy with Buttons.

CHIPPENDALE

Had an accident at the upholsterer's yesterday. Now I'm fully recovered.

JOAN COLLINS

Tuesday

My dearest darling diary. I received a terrible shock today, must have been all that static from those beastly Bri-nylon sheets. Was invited to open the newly built East Lay Chicken Farm, can't think why they asked me.

Wednesday

Felt incredibly vibrant and energetic so I decided to spend the rest of the day in bed.

JAMES CAGNEY

You dirty diary!

Mmn ha, mmn ha, I feel great today—top of the world, ma, top of the world, coz I'm a yankee doodle dandy, yankee doodle do or die. But you dirty diary, you killed my brother, mmn ha, mmn ha, take that—and that—.

AGATHA CHRISTIE

Strange revelations today. The doctor tells me I am pregnant—I must get to the bottom of the mystery but I am almost certain the butler did it.

CASANOVA

Monday

Knackered again. It's exhausting being the world's greatest lover. Everything I touch turns to orgasm. I'm treated like a camel. It's hump, hump, hump, all day long, and the women are just as bad.

Tuesday

Up all night!

Wednesday

Just signed up for the lead in new James Bond film, 'The Man with the Golden Groin'. Refused a part in 'Goldfinger', for obvious reasons. 'Octopussy' was fun though, 'cos I like doing things in eights. Mother called to say she'd had an operation to put in an artificial plastic hip to replace her own hip which was totally worn out. I wonder if they only do hips . . .

Thursday

Got up early this morning. Then later on I got out of bed. Only had a little bit for breakfast, her name was Rosemarie. She scrambled my eggs. Nine more women called round before I had morning coffee. Now I know why it's called elevenses. Went to see a film to take my mind of sex. Unfortunately it was 'Herbie Rides Again'. Thought I'd get an early knight. Sir Rodney came round at 7 pm.

Friday

At last. One whole day of celibacy. For the first time in ages I've been able to cook a sausage and actually use it as food. It's fantastic to be able to look at a packet of fish fingers without having to reach for the vaseline. Today, 'Kay, why jelly?' is just a question about Katherine's choice of pudding. It's marvellous, tonight I sleep only with myself and why not, after all, nobody does it better.

BARBARA CARTLAND

Monday 13th June

His Lordship entered the room. His lean, hungry and erect body lean and hungry in its manly erection. With great languor he languished languidly on the chaise-longue. Although in the autumn of his days, the summery spring in his stride surprised Milady de Winter. Her bounteous bosom heaved heavily. Her big breasts behaved like bouncing bald babies, bobbling in her broderie bodice.

That reminds me, must blow up balloons for the kiddies' party.

Tuesday 14th June

It was a magnificent sight. The beast held his proud head high, his yellowing teeth straining against the bit. Rivulets of sweat poured across his haunches as the rider's crop bit viciously into the muscular rump. The small tail twitched between the beast's heavy hind quarters as Lady Marjorie dismounted. His Lordship collapsed, exhausted on the floor . . .

That reminds me, dinner with Judge Williamson at 8.00 pm.

Wednesday 15th June

It was a dank October day. The last days of summer finally gone. All nature was weary from her months of growth and now she lay still like an old woman, supine, barren. The dry, lifeless leaves tumbled from the trees like the last few hairs on an old woman's scalp.

That reminds me, must get a new hairdresser.

D CHARLES DICKENS

Monday 22nd June

Today has been a day of much personal effort in my perpetual quest to help those in society who cannot help themselves. In the morning I went to the Soot Factory, Emphysema Street. This very profitable enterprise is owned by a friend and fellow philanthropist, Frederick Foreskin. In primitive conditions, child labour is used to bleach soot white, a capital idea! Sucking soot all day furnished the children with a regular diet and they were paid a halfpenny a year for their efforts.

Upon arrival at the refinery I found my old friend in his office. He rose from his desk to greet me, what a pleasure it was to warmly shake Foreskin by the hand again. He was a wealthy man despite being cut off by his father at an early age and was generous to a fault.

He had recently introduced a new scheme for the education of the children. The boys were taken each evening by Mr. Ben Dover and the girls were given oral French lessons by a Miss Jocelyn Grimdyke. Much as I would loved to have lingered I had pressing business to attend to.

My next port of call was the Orphan School for Boys Who Need The Daylights Thrashing Out of Them in Beds. The staffroom was full of familiar friendly faces. The headmaster, Mr De Sade, would spend many hours whipping the boys into shape. A kinder man I have never known, a man who always upheld the school motto 'Bene spankus bottomus', you have to be cruel to be kind.

In the corner of the room was his deputy, Roger Wildly. He used to take the poor mites riding, he enjoyed himself immensely, even though everybody knew he was really flogging a dead horse. Next to him was Mr Peter Phial, the English teacher, a conscientious man who was often rewarded with imaginative sentences. Usually 4–6 years with seven other cases to be taken into consideration.

A recent addition to the staff was the slightly eccentric games teacher, Mr Hitler. He was a short, charismatic man who was immersed in his occupation. A stickler for hygiene, he made sure the boys showered regularly. How happy I was to see these poor orphans in such safe hands.

Returning home from such travels I fell to my bed and into a heavy slumber. As my heavy lids closed and dreamland enfolded me, all I could hear was the comforting sound of rubber against leather.

JAMES DEAN

God, I'm so confused, I love my parents but I hate my Mum and Dad. I love living but I hate life. Jesus, what's happening to me? Oh xylophone, surgical truss, ashtray, y-fronts—no-one understands me.

I hate it when people call me kid, I'm a person not a goat. Why, who, what, where, when, how. . . There's so many questions rushing around in my brain. Why do I have to be home at 11 o'clock? Why does Dad blow his top every time I wreck the car? Why do I get big boils in the middle of my back? Why do I go to sleep and wake up in the morning with a mysterious pink cucumber in my pyjamas? What's happening to me?

Mum bawls me out just because I lie in bed until 3 in the afternoon. Christ, she doesn't realise I gotta get to the bottom of this pink cucumber mystery. She keeps trying to get my Dad to tell me the facts of life. Come on, I know you can get a girl pregnant just by putting your hand up her sweater. And I also know you gotta take precautions—so I always wear a glove. Parents, what do they know?

COUNT DRACULA

Still feeling a bit depressed. To make myself feel better I've been hanging upside down so that the blood rushes to my head but that doesn't seem to make any difference. I don't know what's wrong with me, I looked in the mirror and I couldn't see anything at all.

I'm not in bad shape considering I'm 469 next birthday, mind you, the fangs have lost a little bit of their original glint. What would make me feel better is plunging them into the neck of a beautiful virgin. So the Nurses' Home is out of the question. Maybe I'll stay in tonight. Yes! I'll open one of my best bottles of claret, Château Rhesus Negative and listen to Mike Oldfield on the stereo, my favourite–Jugular Bells.

MARQUIS DE SADE

Thrashed myself with a birch twig. Hated it. Doing it again tomorrow.

JOHN DELOREAN

FRIDAY 13th

SNOWED!

CHARLES DARWIN

Thursday
Proved the theory of evolution—well, I'll be a monkey's uncle.

'Gloria—meet Mum and Dad!'

BOB DYLAN

1963

I'm gonna write the words down, that seem so right to me.
I'll write them truthfully, in my diary.
For the diamond–studded hunchback that plays the tuba.
Rocking, reeling rhythms that rattle from my tongue,
These images of song,
Crammed with alliteration and crazy words like scuba.

Hey Mr Diary, I'll write something for you,
There might be a message hidden beneath this nonsense.
Hey Mr Diary, I'll juggle words for you,
Like a leopard-skin jockstrap dancer burning incense.

The one-eyed crow black raven with a tattoo on his wing,
Wears a crown on just like a king, finds it hard to sing
Because his beak has turned to molten butter.
And the paralytic poet preached parables of pop,
He thinks his heart has stopped,
Because he has only got
One foot and that is in the gutter.

Hey Mr Diary, you are always kind,
All my secrets are safe within your pages
And hey Mr Diary, you never seem to mind,
When I write a line, I often am inclined
To forget about metre and I keep on cramming
As many words into a sentence because I
Know that this burning ball they call the midnight world of para-
noia is just a nightmare illusion soaked in kerosene and you under-
stand when I ramble on for a-a-a-a-a-a-ages.

SIR FRANCIS DRAKE

Saturday . . .

What a day I've had. I'd just completed my circumnavigation of the Globe and I was halfway round the London Paladium when I suddenly remembered that I had a game of bowls to play down at Southampton. I leapt on to a passing Cunard Stagecoach and reached the playing fields just in time.

My opponent wanted to discuss my Golden Hind but I just told him the driver was going a bit fast, and left it at that. I slipped into my spare knickers. I did have some tights with me but I don't like to wear them. Well, they're not very flattering. I can't find a way to wear tights that doesn't make you look as if you've got a pound and a half of garlic in there. And, what's more, neither can my wife.

Bowls. We're halfway through this crucial game when who should turn up but the Spanish Armada. And me in my old knickers. I'll never understand the Spanish. Boatload upon boatload of them come here to get drunk, smash the place up, force themselves on our women . . . and I mean they have to force themselves . . . But generally they just cause nuisance. But the Spics'll sit up when I come at them with my newly recruited Army . . . I call them Club 18–30.

SALVADOR DALI

August 3rd . . .

Did a dream of a painting today.

DISRAELI

Saturday

Passed a motion in the House. Victoria not amused.

DESCARTES

Juin trente

Cogito ergo sum = I sink therefore I swim.
I'm pink therefore I'm spam.
I ink before I cram.
Je pense donc je suis.
Failed Latin again.

GRACE DARLING

Picked up a couple of sailors. Took them back to my place.

E.T.

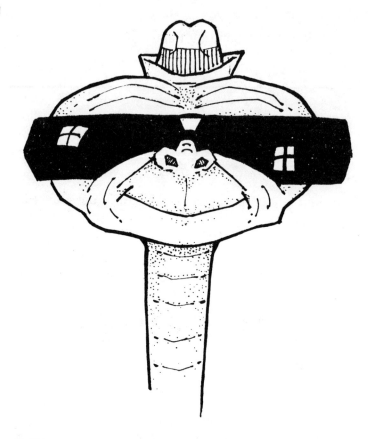

1982

Left behind by spaceship. Taken in and looked after by a little boy in Harlem.

1983

Shi' bro, ain't no fun bein' alien. Dees jive-talkin' human cats ain't nothing mo' than honkies. Technology? Dey don' know shi' man. A guy, he wanna phone home? Dees mothers ain't got nothin' cept two coat hangers and a broken-down set. Cain't make a call an' a cat cain't even get down an' boogie either. Some honky name a Spielberg, he wanna make some movie about me called E.T. I say shoot mother, what's wrong with usin' my real name—Elmer Tyrone? Still, I'll prob'ly do the movie tho', if they get Richard Prior to play me. Man, what a weird-lookin' dude.

Hey, man, just discovered that one of my fingers is magic. No shi'. Everythin' I touch heals up. I ain't never gonna do no heavy pettin' no mo'. Shi'.

THOMAS ALVA EDISON

January 26

Well, I've done it. It took all night and pretty much all morning too—my team of dedicated engineers looking on. And now I've done it. Wife very pleased.

January 27

Invented the word PHONOGRAPH. Now I'm making a fortune printing it on the side of boxes for importing dirty books in.

January 28

Came up with a great invention today. I have invented the world's first electric light bulb. A priceless invention. Can't wait to sell it.

January 29

Dropped it.

January 30

Came up with a great idea for making my fortune out of the light bulb. I invented that little bit of cardboard that goes in the packet and breaks the bulb as you try to get it out.

ELVIS PRESLEY

Decided to meet my rock-a-hula baby, she lives at Heartbreak Hotel way down in the ghetto. But it seems that hard-headed woman is nothing but a devil in disguise, she ain't never gonna love me tender. I told her, 'You're always on my mind and I could spend my whole life through loving you.' I tell you, she's got a wooden heart, ain't no way she's gonna surrender. So I decided it's now or never and tried to put my arms around the big hunk of burning love and do the clam, wow, she's so young and beautiful. She said, 'Don't, don't, don't don't—if you're looking for trouble you've come to the right place.' Then she grabbed me by the Jordanaires and tried to rip it up. Well, there goes my everything.

I just can't help believing she thought I was seeing the girl of my best friend and we sure can't go on together with suspicious minds. Thought it was time for me to go and I stepped out on the street straight into a mess of blue, all over my suede shoes. That Old Shep sure was a hound dog that's a crappin' all the time.

Boy, do I feel way down, I'm feeling so lonesome tonight all I want is for my pelvis to get all shook up. I got the answer, Polk Salad Annie!

ELIZABETH I

November 1558

I've been made Queen. Eat your heart out, Danny la Rue. OK, I admit it. I'm a virgin. So what, with Henry VIII for a father it's enough to put anyone off. I mean take my mum, Anne Boleyn. She had her fair share of nookie and ended up getting her head cut off. Should have been his head, if you know what I mean?

January 1570

I'm definitely developing my own style. I think I'll call it Elizabethan. Lots of half-timbered houses and such. Got an idea for a half-timbered means of transport. Think I'll call it the Morris Traveller.

Still a virgin . . .

June 1588

I stopped Drake from playing with his bowls today. Hey come on, not bad for 1588.

Still a Virgin Queen. Virgin Queen? I wonder if that's a contradiction in terms.

ETHELRED THE UNREADY

(He's gone to get his pencil—Ed.)

EIFFEL

Lying in my bath this morning I had an idea. So I cut my toenails. Ha, only joking, diary, actually I had the idea for what I'm going to build for the Paris exhibition while I was setting on top of a bus . . . but it always happens to me there.

ENGLEBERT HUMPERDINCK

What shall it be? 'Please Release Me'? 'The Last Waltz'? 'Les Bicyclettes de Belsize'? I know . . . I'll call it 'Hansel & Gretel'.

EVE

Adam's in a mood. All I said to him was, 'Do you fancy barbecued ribs for dinner?'

J.R. EWING

Any day I like

Well hi there, diary. Today sure has been one hell of a day, what with all that lying, cheating, corruption, bribery, deception and generally screwing around and all during breakfast as well. Life is so sweet and I'm so damned smug and self-satisfied. Every time I talk to somebody I just can't help being evil and scheming and when I make up another one of my stories, I just have to look to the camera and give one of my confidential smirks. Oo—ee! I could spend all day practising my 'I've just done something sneaky' smile.

When I got to the office I put in a real hard day's work. That's two phone calls, a five-hour lunchbreak and some pistol-shooting practice. I use a picture of Cliff Barnes as a target—I never miss. I won't be happy until that sonofabitch is back in the cow-crap where he belongs. He's gonna die of jealousy when he finds I'm making it with his girlfriend. She's fallen for me coz she loves men who aren't afraid to make it big in the oil business. And I've fallen for her coz she ain't afraid to use the oil business to make it big. That reminds me, I must buy some more shares in Baby Lotion.

Oh well, I suppose I'd better go out and cheat on the wife tonight, got to keep up appearances. I know my brother Bobby disapproves, that damn goody-goody, he's got about as much evil in him as a castrated saint. I think I'll give li'l ol' Marylou a ring, one all covered in gold and diamonds and stuff. Last time I saw her she said the way I walk drives her wild, with them iddy biddy li'l steps an' all. She thought I had to take iddy biddy li'l steps coz I had so much money in my pockets. That's right, honey, I got piles.

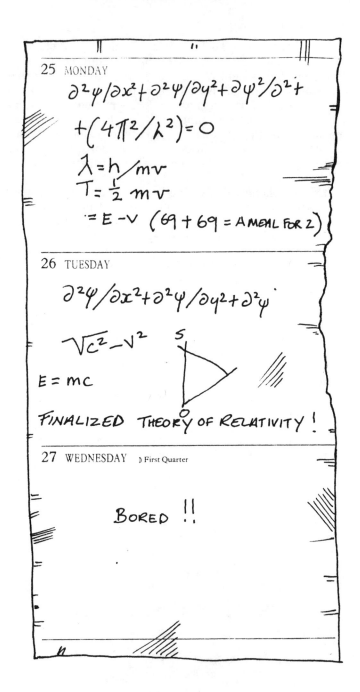

25 MONDAY

$$\partial^2\psi/\partial x^2 + \partial^2\psi/\partial y^2 + \partial\psi^2/\partial^2 t$$
$$+ \left(4\pi^2/\lambda^2\right) = 0$$
$$\lambda = h/mv$$
$$T = \frac{1}{2}mv$$
$$= E - v \quad (69 + 69 = \text{A MEAL FOR 2})$$

26 TUESDAY

$$\partial^2\psi/\partial x^2 + \partial^2\psi/\partial y^2 + \partial^2\psi$$
$$\sqrt{c^2 - v^2}$$
$$E = mc$$

FINALIZED THEORY OF RELATIVITY!

27 WEDNESDAY ☽ First Quarter

BORED !!

F SIGMUND FREUD

Monday

After years of research I have finally decided that all human behavioural problems are deeply rooted in sex. Which explains why so many people are screwed up.

Tuesday

Have decided that an important factor in the development of children's sexual attitudes is potty training. After many experiments I couldn't even get the thing to move never mind jump through a hoop.

Wednesday

10.30 am Oedipus: The poor boy has a complex problem. His problem is his complex. I asked him if he'd ever made love to his mother and he said that she'd been dead for ten years. When I asked him was he a necrophiliac he said no, he'd never been afraid of heights.

Thursday

Made a Freudian slip today. It was in shimmering pink silk with lacy bits of broderie anglaise around the hem. Wore it all day at the office and nobody knew.

Friday

Appointment with my analyst—2 pm.

Saturday

Had a patient today who thought he was Errol Flynn. I told him he had a massive ego, and could I take a polaroid of it?

ERROL FLYNN

SAT.

The sword is mightier than the penis.

W.C. FIELDS

See under Table.

ALEXANDER FLEMING

July 27th . . .

Unfortunately have had diagnosed I have contracted a particularly nasty social disease.

July 28th . . .

Thank God—discovered penicillin.

FRANCIS OF ASSISI

Thursday

I love animals. Case comes up next week. Caught necking with a giraffe, humping a camel and giving a rhino the horn.

MAN FRIDAY

Friday

Met Robinson Crusoe today. He decided to call me Man Friday because we met on a Friday. Good job we didn't meet in a department store or I might have been called Man at C & A.

FRANKENSTEIN

I've got a monster . . . the wife's as pleased as Punch.

'Igor, are you sure you gave him the brain of a criminal?'

JANE FONDA

January 29th

6 am . . . Hup two three four down two three four hup two three four down two three four.

6.15 am . . . Sod it, I'll do the other eyelid tomorrow.

G GUY FAWKES

November 4th

I can't believe it! I spend a hard-earned groat for a tour around the Houses of Parliament and end up lost, stumbling around the vaults in the dark. So what do you do in that situation? Right, you light a match. The next think I know, I was grabbed by the grenadiers, which certainly brought a tear to my eye, and these soldiers lock me up in a cell. So now here I am, awaiting execution tomorrow morning, found guilty of trying to blow up the Houses of Parliament. How did I know the vaults were cram-packed with barrels of gunpowder, I thought they were barrels of beer for a party!

Talking of which, seeing it's my last night, the jailers clubbed together and it didn't half hurt. No, only joking—no, they clubbed together and we had a little shindig. Because it's so cold they made a little fire and we had some baked potatoes and hotdogs to eat. It was nice of the jailers to do all that, if anybody had found us there wouldn't half have been some fireworks. Whatever they are?

GANDHI

'Still no movie deal.'

SAM GOLDWYN

(Include him out—Ed.)

GRETA GARBO

Monday

I wish people wouldn't bother me, I want to be alone.

Tuesday

I wish I could help people, I want to be a loan.

Wednesday

I wish I had a twin sister, I want to be a clone.

Thursday

I wish I had a moment to myself, I want to pee alone.

Friday

I wish I could make my dog happy, I want to be a bone.

Saturday

I wish those three policemen would call again, I want to be alo, alo, alone.

Sunday

I wish I could do a Western, I want to be a Lone Ranger.

Monday

I wish I was in a mental home. I want to be a loon.

PAUL GETTY

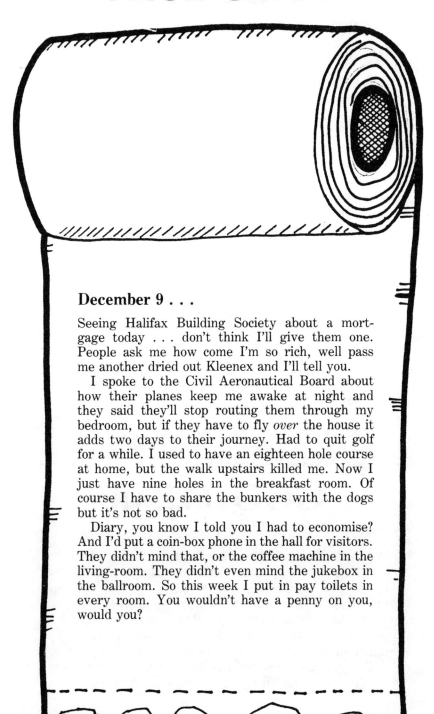

December 9 . . .

Seeing Halifax Building Society about a mort-
gage today . . . don't think I'll give them one.
People ask me how come I'm so rich, well pass
me another dried out Kleenex and I'll tell you.

I spoke to the Civil Aeronautical Board about
how their planes keep me awake at night and
they said they'll stop routing them through my
bedroom, but if they have to fly *over* the house it
adds two days to their journey. Had to quit golf
for a while. I used to have an eighteen hole course
at home, but the walk upstairs killed me. Now I
just have nine holes in the breakfast room. Of
course I have to share the bunkers with the dogs
but it's not so bad.

Diary, you know I told you I had to economise?
And I'd put a coin-box phone in the hall for visitors.
They didn't mind that, or the coffee machine in the
living-room. They didn't even mind the jukebox in
the ballroom. So this week I put in pay toilets in
every room. You wouldn't have a penny on you,
would you?

GOLIATH

BC 230

Went out last night and got stoned.

'Don't try that old sling and shot tripe on me, son!'

GOODYEAR

May 4 . . .

Well, it's one year since I set up the Goodyear Tyre and Rubber Company. Tyres are selling quite nicely thank you because of my great invention . . . the puncture. Unfortunately the rubbers are not going so well. That's because they puncture too. I don't know if you've ever had a blow-out on your condom at eighty miles an hour . . . but it's not a pleasant experience.

The retreads are not taking off as I thought they would—perhaps I'll try that idea on the tyres.

LADY GODIVA

Tuesday
Right, that's it! I've made my mind up. If my husband is going to increase those poor people's rent, I am going to shame him publicly. I'll tell everybody when he gets excited he wets the bed. No, even better, I'll show him what I'm made of, I'll ride naked through the streets as a protest. In fact, I'll show everybody what I'm made of.

Wednesday
Well, I did it, that will show that pig of a husband. Ouch, that horsehair certainly is coarse stuff, mind you, I think I gave as good as I got. We really must do something about those bumpy roads, riding naked has left me with two black eyes.

Thursday
My husband still won't talk to me, he decided to get his own back and ride through the streets naked as well. It serves him right. After five minutes the pain proved too much and he came home with his tail between his legs.

'I admit that the rents are high, but look at the perks we get.'

GERONIMO

1852

First son born today. Saw an elk running. Called boy Running Elk.

1853 . . .

Second son born today. Saw moon rising. Called boy Rising Moon.

1854 . . .

Faulty condom born today.

GILLETTE

January 1st, 1901

Dear Diary, excuse blood, you know my Dad always said that as an inventor I was all thumbs? Well, I took care of that today. I invented the safety razor. Now I'm no thumbs. This is a great invention, if I could only figure out a way to pick it up now.

January 2nd, 1901

Boy will I be a hit with the shavers. For my safety razor I have invented a blade that doesn't rust, go blunt or otherwise wear out. They'll love me. Course the handle breaks first time you use it . . . but what do they expect?

H ERNEST HEMINGWAY

I had things to buy, so I went to a shop, it is called a Manswear shop, a shop where men can buy things to wear. This shop is full of things for men, trousers, jackets, shirts and underpants, you can buy ties there as well—all manner of manly things.

As I entered the shop a man walked slowly towards me, he told me his name was Jones, Mr. Jones. We faced each other, his eyes were gentle but strong, I could tell he had felt much pain in his life. He had the stance of a gentleman's outfitter who had seen many men come and go. His face was proud and bore the lines across his brow that told me more than his name. A face can speak many words, but unlike a mouth it doesn't smell of bad breath.

I told him I wanted trousers. He looked at me and spoke.

'We have many trousers—what colour do you want?'

I told him black, he smiled.

'A wise choice sir, you can't go wrong with black trousers. You are a man who will do well in black trousers, as long as you try.'

It was time for 'the measurementi'—the old way. He took from his neck a five-foot length of plastic, 'the tapo'. It felt good in his hands, years of experience moulded it to his fingers. He knelt before me, like a matador completing his pass as the bull thunders past him. 'Torro'. It was a salute to my machismo, a genuflection of servility that belied his true greatness.

His skilled fingers placed 'the tapo' against the apex of my crotch, his doleful eyes caught mine, I showed no sign of pain. He nodded, we both knew.

'Thirty inches. This is a good inside leg measurementi.'

He went to the rack where many trousers hung, looking like lost souls waiting for bottoms to breathe life into them. I tried a pair on. They were the blackest trousers I had ever seen, blacker than death. They seemed to know me from years long gone and respected the length of my legs and the every contour of my hips and buttocks.

'Are they comfy?' Mr. Jones asked.

'Very,' I replied. 'These are the comfiest pair of trousers yet, you have done well, I must pay you.'

I paid him. As I went to leave he put his hand on my shoulder and handed me a plastic bag.

'Don't you want your old trousers, eh?'

I looked at him, his clear eyes sparkled with honesty, a deep silence fell between us.

'No, you keep them,' I said.

The silence came again, until we both broke into a long and hearty laugh.

I left the shop, the men's shop, a shop where a man can buy trousers as black as death.

HENRY VIII

1520 April

A terrible day. Caught the flu and have been coughing and sneezing all over the place. Wrote new song, thought I'd call it Greensleeves.

1533 May

Lost the only wife I ever loved. Jane Seymour. Bit of a shock when she turned up doing commercials for Max Factor.

Won argument with Thomas More today after he gave me a head start.

Excommunicated by Pope so decided to form my own Church. Cranmer wants to name it after me: The Henry Christian Movement or Harry Chrishna for short. It'll never catch on.

1535 July

Got married again today. Number 6. I think she's called Catherine or something, most of them are. Had the usual banquet then off to bed. I must say it's all very confusing. I don't know if I've had more women or hot dinners. Good luck telegram from Liz Taylor.

Monday

Agreed to marry large-chested German woman.

Tuesday

She's just arrived and she's as flat as a pancake. Must have lost something in translation. Could have sworn they said Anne of Cleavage.

OLIVER HARDY

April 5th . . .

I've got dysentery. Another fine mess . . .

HOWARD HUGHES

Movie business going well. I invented something to show off Jane Russell's attributes to the best advantage. 3-D specs.

Bought a chemstry set. Du Pont.

Flew round the world single-handed. I only wanted to go to Paris. Should've used both hands.

Really into hygiene and cleanliness now. Washed my hands sixteen hundred times this morning. Ooops, have to go to the little boys' room again.

Decided I don't like to be touched. Have issued a memo to all staff and associates to this effect. I can live without being touched by others. Now, where did I put those 3-D specs?

Decided to start wearing shoe boxes on my feet. They are much more hygienic, more comfortable and cheaper than Safeway bags.

Also decided not to cut my nails again. Cutting the nails weakens the body. I made that up. Maybe the nail clippers'll show up.

Important. As of today my organisation will hire only Mormon men. They are clean, trustworthy and I never forget their names. They're all called Elder.

It's now twenty-three years since I stopped cutting my nails. Now I can scratch anywhere I itch.

Memo to entertainment staff. Look, guys, I know I said I only wanted to hire Mormons but I draw the line at the Osmonds.

Explaining my business philosophy to new associate today. I told him, 'You scratch my back and I'll scratch yours' and he ran out of the room.

THE INCREDIBLE HULK

Well, there I was just icing my treacle fancies with a piping
highly regarded by the more up-market of pâtisseries when
I slipped. All that working my fingers to the bone and then
whoosh, a great big dollop flopped out all over my pièce de
résistance. Angry, oo I was. I started to go all green and
burst out of my trousers and shirt. I caught a glimpse of
myself in the mirror and though I say it myself looked quite
a turn-on, all muscley and throbbing. I'm a devil when I'm
roused. Of course I knew it wouldn't last and there I was,
back to normal and in a right state. Well, if my mother had
seen me like that God only knows what she would have said.
So I put my pinny on and had a little tidy-up and then
settled myself down for the evening to put needle and
thread to my tatty trousers. Then blow me if I didn't prick
my finger, pardon my French, and the whole rigmarole
started all over again! What's the point in keeping your
home sweet home spick and span if the next minute it's
going to look like the whole Russian Army have charged
through it without even bothering to wipe their boots. And
another thing, as if it wasn't enough already, that's the fifth
pair of trousers this week! Mind you, I thank God I had the
sense to wear my stretch underpants.

HELEN OF TROY

March 7th . . .

Paris said I have a face that launched a thousand ships. I wish he'd use a bottle of champagne like everyone else.

BENNY HILL

Have invented a new form of musical notation. Here's one of Buddy Holly's greatest:-

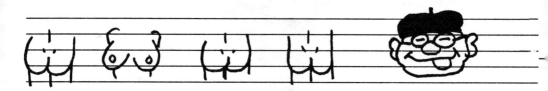

Bum titty bum bum OH BOY

KING HAROLD

'180!'

HITLER

See under Stern magazine

ROBIN HOOD

March 29 . . .

Saw Little John in the forest today. Built hut round it for privacy.

March 30 . . .

Noticed Will Scarlett today. I must be rubbing it too hard.

March 31 . . .

Evil gossip in town about why I'm not fighting in the Crusades. Think about it: would you want a guy who runs around in the forest with a bunch of guys in tights in your army?

April 1 . . .

Got the stuff from the ad agency. They recommend a new name for my gang. The Merry Men. Has a ring to it and it's certainly better than the old name: Robin Hood and the Piss Artists. They've also thought up a new slogan for us: 'They steal from the rich and give to the poor'. Acutally we steal from anybody stupid enough to walk through the forest at night. And when you think about it, what can you steal from the poor anyway?

April 2 . . .

Triar . . . Friar Tuck. Friar Tuck. Friar Tuck. I'll never make that mistake again.

April 3 . . .

Unless I win the Archers Competition, Maid Marian will wed someone else. I'd like to marry her 'cos her old man's got some dough. He runs a very unusual vasectomy clinic in Nottingham.

April 4 . . .

Must win the Archers Competition. Practised all day. It's an everyday story of country folk. It's on at lunchtime then again at teatime. Dan Archer owns the farm. I'll listen again tomorrow.

HEINZ

June 19 . . .

Well, that's it. The jig's up. No more will housewives flock to my store. Somebody told them that Heinz 57 varieties refers to my soup.

Thought of a great new soup today, anyway. My old grandad was incontinent today as usual. I call this one, Cock-a-leekie. Should look nice on the shelf beside the Pea and Ham. What's the difference between Roast Beef and Pea Soup? You can roast beef. Great joke, eh?

But what I really need is a regular line. Something that people will buy all the time. A repeating line. Never mind, I'll think of something. In the meantime my newest invention will keep the company's coffers filled. Tomato sauce . . . of such consistency that you can't pour it out of the bottle, you have to turn the bottle upside down and whack it with the heel of your hand . . . then it all comes out at once and you have to buy another bottle. Great. And it has made me very popular with the Pakistani shopkeepers who like to stay open all night.

HERCULES

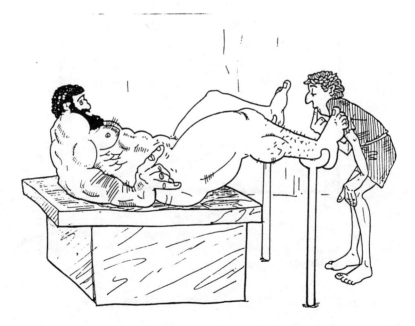

'Are you sure this is one of my twelve labours?'

HOUDINI

IAGO

Tuesday

Oh blackness, oh wounded spirit, oh heart that is as fragile as wardrobe of MFI! How my hatred doth rage within me for my master Othello. For he, Othello, Moor of Venice, most moreish of Moors, the Moor with the mostest, is master of Iago. And so I the sapling, should hew the great oak that is Othello, carve him matchwood and dispatch him to an box of Swan Vestas most profound. And though the rain shall rain and it shall pour over me, no more shall reign no Moor. So Iago goes to lay Othello low, heigh ho.

Wednesday

This morn, as kestrel's cry did crack the dreaming depths of dawn, as suckling babe did nibble teat of mother's breast, as nature's ear was rent by the thousandth flush of loo, did I within my master's mind implant a poisoned seed, which shall grow to poisoned tree as such as Durex doth become balloon. For he doth love a singer of Irish/Italian descent, Des de Mona. She is the sheath of his lusting sword, and cellophane of his manly cigar and the cling-film of his newly-made sandwich. But I, the maggot of jealousy, have eaten into the doubting flesh of his mind. For when he has asked me, 'How goes my dear Des De Mona?' I have said unto him, 'Oh sire, she doth go like a rhino-horned rattlesnake.' And quoth I, 'She doth in the bedchamber a-bonking go with any Thomas, Richard or Henry VI Part II.' Of jealousy, Othello has the signs. Tomorrow, the fruit of my designs.

Thursday

'Tis done. For in the sleeping depth of night, Othello did to Des De Mona's chamber go and there, like Maserati full of choke and throttle, did he strangle his sleeping love. And I, Iago, did laugh in his very face and thrust the barb of hatred to his wounded heart. But, he with majesty and splendour, did forgive me of my deeds and the land did ring to the cries of the people.

> For he's a jolly good Othello,
> For he's a jolly good Othello,
> For he's a jolly good Othello,
> And so say all of us.

CHIEF IRONSIDE

July 11 . . .

Well, I guess I won't be doing any detective work for a long time. I've been shot and my legs are paralysed. Now I can't run. Mind you, that hasn't stopped T.J. Hooker, and at least I have my own hair.

I've got it! I could go around in a wheelchair. Well, why not, there are lots of detectives in LA who have physical disabilities . . . and then there's Barnaby Jones.

I could get a black guy, an Adonis and a nutcase on my squad and we could go everywhere in a van. Wait a minute . . . the A-Team are using the van. I wonder if NCB could stretch to two. Maybe they could rent one.

'Excuse me, but which one of you is Chief Ironside?'

THE INVISIBLE MAN

'Who ordered 30,000 bandages?'

IVAN THE TERRIBLE

Had a Terrible day. Ivan the Noisy came round with Ivan the Necrophiliac who brought his cousin Ivan the Corpse with him. Then a bit later on Ivan the Explosive Device called in with Ivan the Shithouse Door. It's just been bang, bang, bang, all day long. As if that wasn't enough, Ivan the Not Quite Terrible But Still Fairly Nasty called to ask if I'd like to beat his wife up for him because he couldn't cope. So I thought I'd go for a drink down the Prince Ivan when who should walk in but Ivan the Hippy who was so stoned that he tripped over Ivan the Dipso into the arms of Ivan the Throwback who was innocently smashing his head against the corner of Ivan the Fridge Freezer. Went home for an early night. Just my luck the wife was feeling amorous so I had to tell her, 'Not tonight, love, Ivan headache.'

J

JESUS

30 AD

Got a feeling I'm being followed.

JUDGE JEFFREYS

Friday

Had a great day at the bench today. Sent 24 of the bastards to the gallows, that will teach them a lesson they'll never remember. Imagine not knowing the answers to my questions before I had even asked them. Ignorance is no excuse in the eyes of the law.

Straight after work I went to pick up my new car, driving it is almost as much fun as my work. When you turn on the ignition it coughs and splutters so it needs as much choke as possible, then give it loads of throttle; the throttle is my favourite. The brakes are really sharp, so all you have to do is slam them on and the whiplash nearly breaks your neck. The carburettor is specially designed to restrict air supply and the exhaust is falling to pieces; there's nothing like a shattered windpipe.

Fortunately I broke down on the test drive and had to be towed. What absolute pleasure! Being lifelessly suspended at the end of a rope.

JOHN THE BAPTIST

Got a great idea for making sure people believe in the new religion. Hold their heads under water until they come round to our way of thinking. You never know, it could catch on.

Doing a bit of baptism in the river today when Jesus tried to sneak in. I knew who he was immediately 'cos I'd seen His photo on the Shroud in Turin. I told Him I was not worthy to wash His feet, so He washed mine. Glad I didn't offer to execute him, He'd have crucified me. Nice fella. Turns out that His mum knows my mum. Small world . . .

Saw Salome today. She's crazy about me and won't take 'no' for an answer. She just wants everything on a plate. . . Over my dead body.

'No, no! I said, "Bring me the head of John the Baptist." '

JOAN OF ARC

Wednesday

Being taken for a fry-up tonight. Hope I get the steak.

TOM JONES

January 12 . . .

Oh no, I forgot to pack my three extra pairs of socks . . . now what am I gonna stuff down the front of my trousers? I'm getting fed up with this job. I mean, here I am, a grandad . . . I put on trousers so tight you can see my varicose veins through them, stuff half a dozen woollen socks down them and sing 'It's not unusual'. I mean, I'm so old now when I sing that old Frankie Vaughan number in my act it's 'Give me the moonlight, give me the girl and leave the rest . . .'

DR JEKYLL

INDIANA JONES

TOM KEATING

May 4th . . .

Bought a new artist's beret today.

KING KONG

April 19th . . .

Thought I'd do a spot of sightseeing today. Decided to go to the top of the Empire State Building and have a look round. But the way up was crowded. I've never seen so many people. I was surprised. I was going up the outside. You know, from the top you can see all five boroughs of New York. Brooklyn, Queens, Staten Island, Manhattan and the Bronx. Mind you, I'm pretty tough and I can look after myself but I have to tell you, hanging by one hand from the top spire of the Empire State Building is the only way I want to see the Bronx. Well, I'd had lunch before I went up . . . half a dozen humans all with turbans . . . and I'm up at the top, and you know what it's like after you've had an Indian or two . . . an evacuation of the lower tract was called for, urgently. I know they're used to bullshit in NY but I couldn't inflict this on them. Eventually I could wait no longer and I fell off the building. I was fatally injured in the fall and as I closed my eyes I heard someone say 'It was beauty killed the beast.' But it was crap.

'Bandit at 12 o'clock!'

CAPTAIN JAMES T. KIRK

STARDATE: 38-24-36. What a date!
Captain's log—still unable to flush it away.

Myself and a landing party beamed down to an uncharted asteroid to investigate. I knew either I would soon turn into a monster, Spock would fall in love, or Bones would fall into a coma. What could I do? Well, I could dye my hair or hold my stomach in. I decided to do both.

We were approached by a group of strange beings called the Hamericans, aliens that looked like humans in every way, except they were dressed in cheap Hollywood bulk-order costumes. Their leader, a gnarled fossil with skin like parchment, was bent on ruling the universe, he was called Raygun. I had to stop him but first I needed time to think.

I reached for my communicator, a complex signalled device that looked remarkably like a lady's make-up compact, and asked Scotty to beam me up. It was good for me. Spock, the invulnerable Vulcan, pointed out the great danger we were in, with both ears. OK, Spock's arguments were all very logical, but I still couldn't understand why he was wearing black eyeshadow. We contrived a plan that might just work, a plan that was so simple I cursed myself for not thinking of it before. Run away! The chances of Raygun ever ruling the universe were very slim, especially seeing this was only a bit of crazy fiction for kids' TV.

I told Zulu I wanted full speed ahead. I had watched Zulu many times but I was still deeply impressed by Michael Caine's fine performance. We were now up to Warp Factor 8, which is pretty perverted in anybody's language. After consulting my American–Scottish dictionary I discovered Scotty was telling me the engines couldnae take any more. Things got worse. Bones told me he was feeling queasy, I didn't care, he can do what he likes on his night off.

Meanwhile I reeled around the bridge like a drunkard to try and create the impression we were travelling at great speed. Uhuru opened her hailing frequencies and gave me a report, I blame it on the Venusian curry the night before.

Thank God, we were safe. Obviously I was a hero again as Spock and Bones kept calling me Jim; what a couple of creeps, trying to get in my good books. Zulu went back to watching the screen, there wasn't anything good on and the reception was awful, white dots floating around all over the place.

I sat down in my comfortable chair and continued to wrestle with a problem that had been bothering me all that day. Why was I still wearing a pyjama top? I decided it was time to go boldly where no man had boldly gone before.

'Uhuru, report to my cabin—and that's an order!'

RUDYARD KIPLING

October 19 . . .

If you can keep you head when all about you
Are losing theirs and blaming it on you;
If you can trust yourself when all men doubt you,
But make allowances for their doubting too;
If you can wait and not be tired by waiting,
Or being lied about, don't deal in lies,
Or being hated, don't give way to hating,
And yet don't look too good, nor talk too wise;
If you can dream—and not make dreams your master;
If you can think and not make thoughts your aim;
If you can meet with Triumph and Disaster
And treat those two imposters just the same;
You must be on twelve valium a day.

EDWARD KENNEDY

June 3rd

So I said, 'Do you wanna go for a drive or take a swim?' And
she couldn't make up her mind, your honor.

So I said, 'Ok, sir, I admit I paid a guy at Harvard to take a
test for me . . . I didn't think it would hurt since it was only
a blood test . . . for a paternity suit.'

FRANZ KAFKA

Monday

Oh dear, think I've turned into a Beatle.

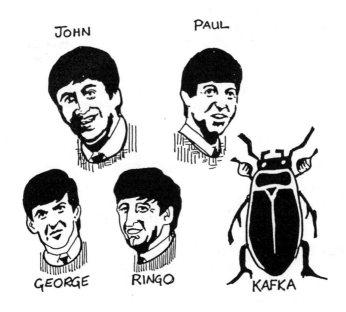

JOHN   PAUL

GEORGE   RINGO   KAFKA

JOHN F. KENNEDY

Monday

Oh dear, think I've turned into an airport. Must stop reading Kafka.

KERMIT THE FROG

April 8th

What a day! As if life is not difficult enough without Jim Henson sticking his hand up my bottom and jiggling me about in front of a television camera. And people are so nasty to me. Take Bob Monkhouse, for instance (I wish somebody would). The other day he was a guest on the show and he asked me what it was like to be made of cheap material. I told him he should know since it was cheap material that had made him.

People don't realise how difficult it is being a Muppet. It's like being a puppet with a harelip. It's not like Sesame Street, with all those nice ethnic, hippy people smiling stupidly and pretending that ghettos are wonderful places to live in and treating the snotty little kids like morons. That was really fun, it's not often that a frog gets to talk down to people. Well, people think I'm a frog, but I'm not really, it's just that when Jim Henson was suffering from a heavy cold one day he coughed, and there I was in his hand. I suppose I'm a product of recycling, which is OK by me because at least it's trendy.

BILLIE-JEAN KING

Monday

Just had a game with my coach. He said, 'You're not doing badly for someone who's pushing forty-love.' I said, 'What the deuce do you mean?' 'Well,' he replied, 'you haven't gone to seed. And anyway, I heard about the services you did for Virginia.' 'Virginia?' I said. 'Wade a minute, you dirty little Okker. I wasn't Bjorn yesterday.'

Tuesday

Bought a new car. Rather a smart racey Austen. Had to Phil a few dents in the bodywork but it's very good around the Connors.

Wednesday

Went to the ball. The ball was good. New car broke down—had to borrow one. My friend Ivan Lendled it to me.

Thursday

Feeling Illie today. Went to the doctor. He says I've got a Nastase case of Geruilaitis Navratilova—the Goolagongs. Only hurts when I go for a Slazenger. Hope I don't Buster Mottram.

KITCHENER

November 6th . . .

Got it at last. It's been up my right nostril for the last two weeks.

L JOHN LE CARRE

I sat alone in the saloon bar of the Birch and Bottom Public House. A bar frequented by an army of charcoal-grey pinstripes of the Civil Service, and sometimes even civil servants themselves. Civil servants, or as they call themselves, secret servants. The gin and tonics rang to the memory of England's finest, Philby, Burgess, Maclean, Freeman, Hardy, Willis.

The little bald man with the sad eyes which told nothing and yet said everything trudged wearily towards my table.

'George, old darling, old thing, old man, old love,' I said, using his code name. 'How's Anne?'

His sadness seemed more intense at the mention of his errant wife. 'Anne is fine,' he replied. 'Vladimir is dead. He knew Karla's daughter was in Paris. The Russians had the safe house but the Cousins turned their agent. The Paymaster was a sleeper. Hayden was a double and the cover was blown on the dead letter box.'

'But what about the mole in the circus?' I asked.

'Don't worry,' he said, 'I've got the tickets.'

'How's Connie?' I asked.

'Connie's fine,' he said. 'Lacon says the opposition have brought in Karla-trained-China-watchers. Good tradecraft, poor intelligence. The whole operation is strictly hush on a need-to-know-basis.'

'But,' I asked, 'what about the SE Asian theatre?'

'Don't worry,' he said, 'I've got the tickets.'

'How's Guillam?' I asked.

'Guillam's fine,' he said. 'Moscow centre's honeytrap has taken Lamplighters out of the game. My masters at the FO have the negatives, thanks to Scalphunters.'

'But what about the Treaty?' I asked.

'For Christ's sake,' he yelled, 'I'm already taking you to the circus and the theatre, what more do you want?'

LEONARDO DA VINCI

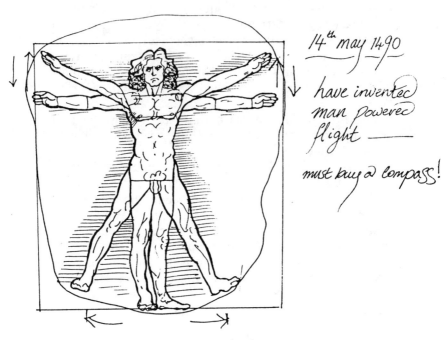

14th may 1490

have invented
man powered
flight —

must buy a compass!

'You do the Okey-Cokey and you shake it all about. . .'

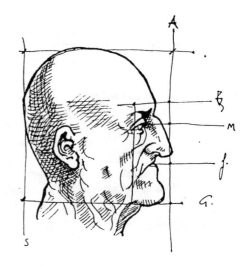

15th may 1490

finished designs
for new invention! —

will call it —

Spectacles !!

16th May 1490

have invented an underwater machine.
will call it

The TITANIC !!

Leonardo.

EDWARD LEAR

There once was an Edward called Lear,
Whose poems gave people much cheer,
The metre and rhyme,
Were truly sublime,
So they forgave him for being so queer.

ABRAHAM LINCOLN

April 14th

Need to go to the theatre tonight like I need a hole in the head.

LONG JOHN SILVER

June 22nd . . .

Arrr, shiver me timbers an' fasten me fo'c'sle. Strap me leg on and drop me anchor, aaaahhh. Polly's messed on me coat again, arrr, and she keeps biting me crutch, arrr. Still, she's a lovely girl, arrrr.

We were three days out of port and the rum was getting low as well, arrrr. The bosun dished out thirty lashes to the crew, and them that couldn't have lashes got extra mascara . . . or is it cascara, I can never remember. I soon find out, though, arrr.

The crew were punished because they made fun of me. They ridiculed my peg leg and my eye patch and the hook I have for a hand, arrr. And it's only my first voyage. I accept I look frightening to some and a figure of fun to others . . . but I get enough of that from the pasengers.

Found a stowaway today. He begged and pleaded that I keep his presence secret from the others, arrr. Didn't have the heart to tell him this was the Woolwich Ferry.

LONGFELLOW

Saturday

Completed my epic poem, 'Higher Watha'.

'I said, "Could you read us another of your poems?" '

THE LONE RANGER

Sept. 28th

Hi ho, as usual trying to capture some wrongdoer or other. Today I'm looking for the sonofabitch who put black ink on the inside of my sunglasses.

I really am a lonely lone ranger since I sacked Tonto yesterday. That guy has been calling me kimosabi for the last twenty years and I only just found out it was Apache for bumface. Cheek! Tonto is now back on the reservation enjoying himself. He spends all his time bent on one knee scratching maps in the dust with a stick for anyone who is crazy enough to take notice.

Silver, my horse, threw a shoe last night. I only tried to kiss her. I gotta meet a gal soon and settle down, that horse is getting more goddamned attractive every day.

M THE MARX BROTHERS

Saturday

GROUCHO

Met Mrs. Windermere and Mr. Pasternak. Mrs. Windermere, Mr. Pasternak, Mr. Pasternak, Mrs. Windermere. Mrs. Windermere, Mr. Pasternak, Mr. Pasternak, Mrs. Windermere, etceteri, etcetera, etceteri, etcetera.

We all had dinner. OK, we had dinner but there's no need to make a meal of it. We all had hors d'oevres. I ate the d'oevres and Mrs. Windermere had the horse. Remind me to give her a nosebag next Christmas. Mr. Pasternak wanted his steak well grilled, I questioned it for three hours and still didn't get a confession. I gave it the third degree and now it's the most qualified steak au poivre you ever met. Wow, could that Mrs. Windermere eat, for dessert she ordered the Sahara.

Before I left, I gave Mrs. Windermere a gift, a little something to remember me by. The bill. Goodnight Mrs. Windermere, Mr. Pasternak, etceteri, etcetera.

CHICO

Wassamatta? We ain'ta gotta no money? Don'ta matta.
I see the lona ranger. No! Notta the lone ranger—the
loan arranger. Never mind. That's irrelefant. But if
it's irrelefant it shoulda be in a zoo. Don'ta worry, I
gotta diary here. Hey if I gotta diary here, I better go
see a doctor.

HARPO

Honk, honk, honk! Whistle, whistle! Honk! Whistle!
Honk, honk!

KARLO

The means of honk honk production whistle is honk
whistle controlled by the honk whistle workers.

MAX MILLER

July 11th . . .

Listen, diary . . . no, listen . . . I got up . . . no, I did . . .
I'd just got up . . . then she had to go home . . . listen . . .
you'll get me in trouble, missus . . . now, I did . . . I got up,
went out and . . . blow me down, if they weren't selling
strawberries . . . no, listen, they were . . . so I said to the
girl, I'll have a pound . . . an' she pounded me . . . no, wait,
missus, she did . . . anyway, I eats the strawberries . . .
one at a time, I'm not greedy . . . and . . . 'ere, missus, do
you know the blokes sitting either side of you . . . what???
. . . sorry, I thought you 'ad two heads up yer jumper . . .
now, I eats the strawberries . . . and I'm walking home . . .
when suddenly, I get this strange feeling in me . . . you
know, missus . . . me trousers . . . no, I did, listen . . . so I
rush to the doctor's . . . he says, drop your trousers . . . so I
do . . . and . . . wait . . . and he says . . . now there's a
funny thing . . . I'm not kidding . . . he says, What caused
that, Max? . . . 'cos I knew him . . . I said, Strawberries
. . . he said, Strawberries? . . . I said Strawberries. He
said, I'll give you some cream to put on them.

MCARTHY

April 30th . . .

Just take a look in your back pages, diary, can't be too
careful, them Red Pinkos are everywhere . . . My phone is
bugged, my car is bugged . . . even my bed is bugged and
when I went to my dancing class even my shoes were
tapped.

JOHN MERRICK

Today I met the most simply wonderful lady. She's not like the others, who take one look at me and scream hysterically and have to be carted off to the nearest mental institution. In fact, I think she might be sexually attracted to me. She said I was the most amazing person in the sack she had ever met and fully understands why I'm called The Elephant Man.

NORMAN MAILER

42nd October

Concrete jungle, sex, sex, more sex, needle shower spray relaxing taut muscles, ambition, drive, hard liquor, more sex, more liquor, 22nd storey balcony, liquor licker, lick her deep, kiss, make a million, country home, wild party, acrid taste of nicotine on her breath, breasts, firm thighs, Marilyn, diamonds, dollars, double deal, dope, drugs, swindle, affair, love, heartbreak, stream of conciousness, money for old rope, sex, sex, life, death, life, death, full stop.

MIDAS

May 14th . . .

Everything I touch turns to gold. Dying for a leak.

JOHN McENROE

Had a very traumatic press conference today. Some of the journalists suggested I was spoilt, immature and childish. I told them that I wasn't and if they dared to say it again I was going to go straight home and tell my mom.

Beat Jimmy Connors. I hit the balls harder than him. Must try playing tennis with him sometime.

THREE MUSKETEERS

LUNDI

WHAT A DREADFUL DAY WE'VE HAD
WHAT A DREADFULL DAY WE'VE HAD
WHAT A DREADFUL DAY WE'VE HAD

IT'S NOT ALWAYS FUN DOING THINGS IN THREES
IT'S NOT ALWAYS FUN DOING THINGS IN THREES
IT'S NOT ALWAYS FUN DOING THINGS IN THREES

ASK MY WIFE, AS SHE ALWAYS SAYS, TWO'S
ASK MY WIFE, AS SHE ALWAYS SAYS, TWO'S
ASK MY WIFE, AS SHE ALWAYS SAYS, TWO'S

COMPANY, THREE'S A PHYSICAL IMPOSSIBILITY!
COMPANY, THREE'S A PHYSICAL IMPOSSIBILITY!
COMPANY, THREE'S A PHYSICAL IMPOSSIBILITY!

MARDI

THE DEODORANT CONTRACT CAME THROUGH
THE DEODORANT CONTRACT CAME THROUGH
THE DEODORANT CONTRACT CAME THROUGH

FOR ARAMIS TODAY. SO NOW WE DON'T SAY
FOR ARAMIS TODAY. SO NOW WE DON'T SAY
FOR ARAMIS TODAY. SO NOW WE DON'T SAY

'EN GARDE' ANYMORE WE SAY, RIGHTGUARD!
'EN GARDE' ANYMORE WE SAY, RIGHTGUARD!
'EN GARDE' ANYMORE WE SAY, RIGHTGUARD!

MACBETH

December 4th . . .

After yon battle today I again laid eyes on those three witches. Down in the Falklands they get Jim Davidson. We get the Beverley Sisters.

Anyway, I'll get a bit of peace now, they're not coming back until the summer. I heard them say they won't meet again until 'thunder lightning or rain.'

Got a busy night. King Duncan's coming over and I've got to kill him. I'm already Thane of Glamis and I could be Thane of Cawdor. But I'd rather be king. At least I know what that is.

Ach, I walked in tae Duncan's chamber . . . it was a stupid place tae leave it . . . and I went tae stab him with mah big dagger, but I couldn't bring myself to do the evil deed . . . he was wearing my pyjamas.

Lady Macbeth said do it. Or she would. Anyway, he'd dead now and then I remembered that Banquo had heard the witches tell me that I could be king . . . so just in case he put two and two together and made five . . . I killed him, too.

This place is haunted now. And old Lady MacB is looking daggers at me as if it's my fault. Never mind. I'm king, my castle is haunted . . . now if only I had a monster in the loch I could open to the public.

'Is this a Jagger I see before me?'

MORSE

January 19th . . .

Really lubbered myselp this tibe. Had a call frob de Presidebt about cobbubicatiobs and he asked be to helb. I told hib I had a code ab he bisuberstood be.

January 20th . . .

Better today. And I think I've solved the problem of the code I'm meant to come up with. How's this?

$$\cdot\ \cdot\ \cdot\ -\ -\ -\ \cdot\ \cdot\ \cdot$$

Great isn't it? I got the idea from my dog after he'd chewed the bones from my leftover chicken vindaloo.

January 21st . . .

Got it. The rest of this will be in my new Morse Code. Dot. Dot dot dash dash dot dot dot dash dash. Dash dot dot dot dash dash dot dot dot dot dot dot dash dash dash dot dash dash dot dot dot dash dash dash dash. Dot dot dot dot dot dot dot dot oh dash dot dash. Dosh dat dosh dat drat dish dot dash.

January 22nd . . .

$$-\ \cdot\ -\ -\ \cdot\ \cdot\ -\ -\ \cdot\ -\ \cdot\ -\ \cdot\ -\ \cdot\ -\ \cdot\ \cdot$$

MENDEL

Sunday

After years of observation and calculation I have at last discovered the secrets of inheritance, the natural laws which govern heredity. One thing still puzzles me, though. I have three sons, two of whom are as like as peas in a pod but the third tends more towards the pansy variety. My two sons who are as like as peas in a pod give me great comfort as I watch them working hard tilling the fields. What a glorious sight, just to watch them, with their gleaming green skin, brilliant blue hair and muscular, eight-foot tall bodies. It makes you proud to be a father.

MOSES

Long Time Ago in BC in Egypt

Plagues and more plagues. As if the locusts weren't bad enough, now we've got a plague of frogs. They're absolutely everywhere with their big noses, smoking their foul cigarettes and drinking UHT milk. Furthermore, the Plague of the Death of the First Born didn't do much good because Donny and Marie Osmond have got an elder brother.

Bit Later BC

Went to the Burning Bush. Had a few pints. I started to hear voices. Better lay off the hooch.

Later Still BC

Went up the mountain for a chat with God. He asked if I wanted any commandments. I said, 'How much are they?' He said, 'They're free.' 'OK then,' I said, 'I'll take ten.' Had a headache but felt much better after I took the tablets.

'What would you like, a centre or a side parting?'

NAPOLEON

Monday
Josephine tonight.

Tuesday
Josephine twice tonight!

Wednesday
Josephine three times tonight.!

Thursday
not tonight, Josephine!

NERO

Janus 12us

Funny burning smell in Rome this morning. I smelled it last night and I thought the people and the senate of Rome were having a barbecue without inviting me—their illustrious leader and resident pyromaniac. What colour! What light! Eat your heart out, Blackpool. I don't think they can blame me for this. I may have lit the fire but I didn't create the climate of decadence . . . well, yes, I suppose I did. Some members of my government say that I am an unfair and reactionary ruler. They won't say that again . . . I've had them put to death.

LORD NELSON

Dear Diary, tomorrow I will fight the greatest battle of my life. My final attempt to overthrow the ambitions of the tyrant. And then, when I get out of Emma's bed, I must go and fight the Battle of Trafalgar. I am worried. I told Emma I have a great foreboding. She said she wasn't complaining. In my last two battles at sea I have lost an arm and an eye. What will I lose tomorrow? Perhaps I will become the world's first vasectomy patient.

Fear not, my faithful Diary, for I shall not flinch in my duty towards my country. I have two messages that will both inspire the fleet and be remembered by stout-hearted Englishmen for centuries to come. The first is 'England expects every man to do his duty' and the second, 'Have you heard the one about the Mother Superior and the randy donkey?' Guaranteed to bring tears to the eyes. I know that during this battle I shall be afraid, but I shall show no fear. I shall merely slowly walk back and forth in that place where so many have been frightened before me, the poop deck, knowing that I alone am responsible for all the seamen around me, and the whole messy business is entirely in my hands.

I am weary now, I must sleep. Tomorrow I shall succeed or my name is not Lord Nelson. I wonder why mother named me after a pub in Barnsley?

NIJINSKY

June 5th

What a fantastic day. Not only danced the pas de deux from 'Les Sylphides' by Délibes with Margot Fonteyn but I came third in the 3:30 at Ascot as well.

ISAAC NEWTON

Day 1

Day 2

Day 3

Day 4

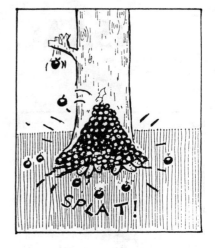

Day 5   *Day 6*

'Made an important discovery today—invented cider.'

NARCISSUS

Spring

Dear Diary, can you keep a secret? Cross your heart and hope to become an address book? Well, you know I've spent all day stuck like a fool down by the lake gazing at the most gorgeous creature that ever walked the earth in a pair of kidskin slingbacks? It's all off between us! Of course it started off fine, I'd smile at him, he'd smile back, then I'd give a little wave, then he'd give a little wave. Well, I kept this up all day long. I was sure it was the real thing, then the first sign of rain and he buggers off!

Anyway, I saw his double on the way home, in a shop window. I think he likes me, he followed me home. And every window I looked into, there he was giving me the glad-eye.

FLORENCE NIGHTINGALE

April 16 . . .

I am very disappointed to find that critics of my hospital here in the Crimea are suggesting that my nurses and I are interested only in the bodies of the men we help and not the care and cure of those unfortunates. I had a strict and sheltered upbringing . . . but to suggest that I am obsessed with men's bodies appals me. You could've knocked me down with a big—I don't know what it's called—when I heard it. I am prepared to admit that some of my girls are so obsessed, however, and I do have one nurse who in our first day here performed sixty-nine enemas . . . and we only had one patient then. I am more concerned with the cruelty of some of the staff I have inherited. Now, I am perfectly aware that all nurses and even doctors have little inoffensive tricks they like to play on patients. Like keeping the stethoscope in the ice bucket and the anal thermometer in the pepper pot . . . all harmless fun . . . but I have had to admonish my matron who was overheard saying to a pathetic double amputee, 'Do you want the good news or the bad news first? Her bedside manner leaves a lot to be desired. I am having to sack some of the more malicious girls but I have assured them that after training there will be futures for all of them in the field of medicine. They can all be doctors' receptionists.

April 17 . . .

The castor oil arrived today. Talk about the relief of Mafeking.

'Nurse Nightingale! I think you are taking this "Lady of the Lamp" business a little too far!'

NOAH

'Must make sure there's two of everything.'

NUREYEV

Saturday

Today is the grand opening of 'The Nutcracker'. I hope I made the right decision to have a vasectomy.

JAMES BOND 007

I awoke this morning in an upright position, as usual I was ready for anything. Sabrina, the beautiful Russian spy, ran her fingers through my hair. There was no time for that, I needed my toupé back on my head where it belonged. I remembered the passion of the night before, when her ripe breasts had exploded into my hands—even her bra was booby trapped! Meanwhile, Sabrina lay back in bed and pulled long and hard on a Black Russian. God knows what he was doing there. Who was she working for? The CIA, the KGB, MI5? I had an itchy feeling it was THRUSH.

Within the hour I was at HQ being debriefed. They said they would return my underpants later. I walked into M's office. Talking to M was a tall, thin man whom I recognised as Jonny Fetherlite, a slippery customer if ever I saw one. M explained that our arch enemy Number 2 had surfaced again and was up to his old tricks and had to be stopped at all costs. I would have to go alone as Fetherlite had blown his cover. I knew that handling Number 2 would be a messy business but it was a big job and it had to be done. To help me in this mission M had a new plastic explosive cleverly disguised as a rope. He slipped me a length.

When I arrived at Number 2's secret hideout I vaulted the electric fence in a single leap and then killed the guard with a chop to the throat. A leg of lamb would have been more efficient but my deep freeze supplies were running low. I then placed and primed the explosives and escaped like the wind along the back passage. The hideout went up in a great ball of fire that even Jerry Lee Lewis would have been proud of.

Mission accomplished I returned home. After all that effort, tension and concentration I needed to relax, I decided to slip into something a little more comfortable. Fortunately, Sabrina was still in the bedroom.

OEDIPUS

Today has been a nice day. The sun was in the sky. The birds were singing. Mummy and Daddy took me on a picnic. We went by the river. It was nice. It was good. Mummy gave me some lemonade. I love my Mum. Daddy ate all the sandwiches. I hate my Dad. And when I am big and strong I will kill him. That will serve him right. And when I am grown up I will marry my Mum. Coz she is lovely and she is kind and she's got great tits and the best arse I've ever seen. The end.

ONAN

Wednesday

Thought for one terrible moment today that I had become impotent . . . but it was just my hand had gone to sleep.

ORPHEUS

See under World.

DONNY OSMOND

Mormonday, April 6th . . .

Getting married tomorrow.

April 7th . . .

Getting married tomorrow.

April 8th . . .

Getting married tomorrow.

April 9th . . .

Getting married tomorrow.

April 10th . . .

Getting married tomorrow.

April 11th . . .

Don't think I can take much more of this, I'm not used to it . . .
Five stag nights in one week. Wives are complaining I don't show
much interest in them anymore. I go to bed just after seven each
night and number eight isn't too pleased, I can tell you. Women.
They're more trouble than they're worth.

April 12th . . .

Getting married tomorrow.

OBERON—King of the Fairies

Monday

What do I have to do to get just a little respect? Everybody I meet it's the same old story. 'What's your name?' they ask, 'Oberon,' I say. 'Oo, that's a good name. What do you do for a living?' 'I'm the King of the Fairies,' I say. Hoots of derision and gales of laughter. Then of course they start on the jokes, don't they? 'King of the Fairies, I'd have thought Queen of the Fairies was more appropriate' or 'I bet you can't wait to get to the bottom of my garden. Or would you prefer to garden my bottom?'

Why is it that people assume that because one is a fairy then one is automatically gay? Why can't there be such a thing as a butch fairy? I mean, look at Burt Reynolds. I'm very happily married to my wife Titania. She calls be Obe for short, and of course I call her Ania.

Tuesday

Saw Puck today. I sent him on a special assignment. He put a girdle around the earth in forty minutes, which is more than I could do for Russell Grant. Puck was trying it on again, but I wasn't having any. I told him in no uncertain terms, 'Puck, off.'

Wednesday

Sat on a toadstool—apologised to the toad.

PICASSO

2nd february 1940

still can't draw faces !!

Pablo

DOLLY PARTON

May 22nd

Well lawdy lawdy, beat my butt with a black-eyed hickory stick, if that just don't beat all. I just seem to be running around in circles doing nothing but making a lot of butter. Today I released a 45, those bras are useless, took me half an hour with a shoehorn to get it back in there again. Then it took another half an hour to tie my shoelaces.

By the time I was dressed it was lunchtime so I had a salad sandwich and a large jug of milk. Mama always said you'll need large jugs if you wanna get on in showbiz. Put me in mind of those early days at those Nashville concerts, I'd just stand there all day keeping the rain off the audience. Those were sad days, like when I lost my first husband. I dropped an earring down my cleavage, he tried to get it back for me and has never been seen since.

I got that crazy sculptor coming round this afternoon who is going to immortalize li'l ol' me in stone. A bust that will go down in history.

GENERAL PATTON

August 30th . . .

Fighting with the Seventh Army now. I can't get on with anyone.

SAINT PETER

Forever

Another hard day at the Gates of Heaven. I some-times think I'd be better off on earth. Down there at least I was Pope, up here I'm just a lousy doorman. And they call that going up in the world. Yeah, being Pope wasn't so bad. OK, so I had to run around in a skirt and speak in a language nobody understands but at least the job had perks. Unlimited cash, women, booze. It's a great way to see the world. So, I die, and what do I get as a reward for being the rock on which the church was built? He makes me a bloody commis-sionaire. 'Welcome to Heaven, sir. Carry your harp, sir? Have a nice eternity now.' I'm sure he's never forgiven me for denying him thrice before the cock crowed.

Later

Business has been a bit slack lately. Judging by the number of people getting in 'downstairs' things must be really swinging on earth. With all those queues it must be Hell down there. Old Satan's getting all the classy trade—Methodist ministers, Roman Catholic Archbishops—whilst all we get up here are burnt-out rock 'n' roll singers and groups of 3 who always turn out to be an Englishman, and Irishman and a Scots-man.

Later Still

Went into voluntary liquidation today. Macdonalds take over tomorrow.

ISAAC PITMAN

May 4th . . .

Today I opened my college where young ladies will come to learn how to be secretaries. It was a long hard day. We had thirty-six pupils and my lap is numb. We went through basic secretarial skills . . . like typing a letter containing two hundred words without spelling one word correctly, filing important letters in such a way that they will never be found except by accident, and varnishing nails. Some of the girls complained about my shorthand method. I appologised but told them they shouldn't dress provocatively.

Went to the park at lunchtime to relax, get my mind together for the afternoon and to look up girls' dresses. I was by the pond when I espied a young lad with a marmalade jar full of tadpoles all wriggling about and I had this brainwave for a universal shorthand language.

The Pitman Shorthand Method

JACKSON POLLOCK

EDGAR ALLAN POE

Friday 13th

Last night I awoke in the middle of the night. There were beads of pespiration on my brow and the sheets were wringing wet—damn that leaky colostomy bag. I had dreamt a dream riddled with terrifying guilt, a guilt that burned deeply inside me, a guilt that consumed me slowly, painfully, guiltily. What a horrible dream it had been, a dream of unspeakable horror that had been horrifyingly horrific.

Had it really been this hand that had picked up the cleaver and mercilessly hacked the body, chopping it to pieces and then carefully placing them in plastic bags? Was it I who had washed away the congealing blood matted with splinters of bone so carefully, not leaving a clue behind? Was I the one who had hidden the recently dismembered carcase in the freezer, hoping to dispose of it later, piece by bloody piece? I had to find out the truth. Whether this was all some kind of crazy revolting dream or an unforgivable act that would damn me to burn in the fires of hell for eternity.

I walked towards the kitchen. In the eerie half light my imagination played tricks on me and I swore I could hear a faint heartbeat coming from the place where I had committed the heinous act. Before me I saw the chest where I had deposited the body, a chest that now so much resembled a coffin. The sound of the heartbeat increased, a steady surging that rang so accusingly in my ears. As I opened the door of the chest the room was flooded with light. I looked inside.

O God—it was true! For there, still sealed in their ghastly grim packages, were the legs, shoulders, stomach and ribs; a confetti of carnage. I fell to my knees and prayed as I have never prayed before. O God, why me! Why should I be the one chosen to be your friendly family Dewhurst butcher?

PASTEUR

May 2nd . . .

What an incredible breakthrough! I have discovered that it is possible to attenuate the virulence of injurious micro organisms by exposure to air, by variety of culture or by transmission through various animals. And I wouldn't know that if I hadn't had a Big Mac at lunchtime. I have been experimenting with sheep and cows . . . but enough of my personal life . . .

It's all very well having my own institute and being able to spend all day studying putrefaction, lactic fermentation butyric fermentation and even acetic fermentation . . . but try getting the milkman to deliver.

PAVLOV

Have at last completed my research into stimulus response that I have been conducting with a group of dogs. Before I feed them I ring a bell. Slowly they have come to associate the sound of the bell with their feeding time and therefore start to salivate. The problem is, this morning the phone went and I was up to my neck in dog-flob.

PEPYS

Never heard of him!—Ed.

Q QUILT

See under Duvet.

QUASIMODO

January 7th . . .

Went to the barber's today . . . look a lot better since he took a bit off the back.

Q

Monday

Today, Bond walked into my office. I showed him a highly sophisticated ingenious device especially designed to help him in tight corners. It's called a vibrator. This piece of hardware is particularly effective in getting foreign agents to talk, and, on certain occasions, scream. Bond asked what to do in the case of a full body search and I told him: You know where you can stick it.

Tuesday

Received a report from Bond today. Using the vibrator he has debriefed Ivan Czestikov, undercover agent and principal dancer in the Bolshoi Ballet. Ivan has demanded political asylum and a new set of batteries.

R OLIVER REED

Monday

Went out, got drunk, beat up some geezers. Got drunker, beat up some other geezers. Got home, made an omelette, beat up some eggs.

Tuesday

Appointment with hairdressers, touch up roots on chest hair.

RÖNTGEN

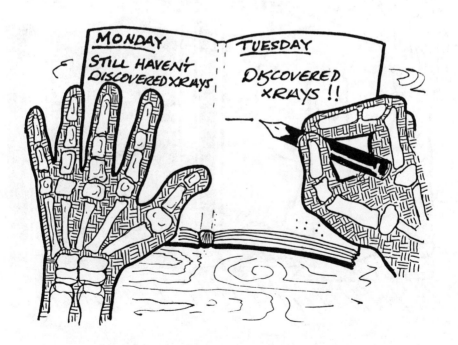

W HEATH ROBINSON

WALTER RALEIGH

Alas and alack, I find myself imprisoned in the Tower of London. I have been here these three years and thirty-seven days—almost as long as some of the tourists in the queue outside.

I was sent here by that little Scottish fairy, James the First . . . or Jimmy the Sax as they call him in Edinburgh—because he likes a good blow. I am led to believe that my imprisonment is a result of my unsuccessful expedition to the Orinoco . . . I could've sworn he lived near Wimbledon . . . but I know the real reason: because I am opposed to the introduction of the Official Bible. What a load of old twaddle it is. 'Get thee behind me Satan' indeed. I had enough of that in the Navy.

James was upset when he asked me who had supplied the loaves for the Sermon on the Mount and I said it was J. Hovis.

Still, here I am, in the Tower. One small window, stone floor, freezing cold in winter and no air in summer. Mind you, it's miles better than my Barratt's house.

I've decided to write the History of the World, Part 1. I sent an outline to the publishers. They wrote a nice letter back asking me to choose another subject.

So, here I am, in the Tower. I can't understand why they queue up to get in here. I suppose it's to view the Crown Jewels. Of course, I've seen those in a very intimate situation. On the night table beside the glass with the teeth in.

We're really close, me and the Queen. Oh yes. I'm her favourite. When I was in America I even named a State after her: Ducksarse. Actually, we changed it to Virginia just in case I wanted to live there.

I did live there for a while and I discovered an item which has been the subject of much controversy in this country. Should we, shouldn't we? Is it anti-social? Is it harmful? Who cares??? Just ask yourself this one question: what would shepherd's pie be without it?

And I introduced tobacco. That's another reason why we changed the name of the region to Virginia. Who's gonna put Ducksarse tobacco in their mouth? Yeah, well, apart from James I.

What a discovery that was. Not only does the Treasury benefit from the tax on smokers but there's all the taxes derived from spin-off businesses. Match makers, ashtray makers and 'NO SMOKING' sign manufacturers.

But somehow I managed to end up in the Tower. What an ending for a man of my ilk. Left to starve in a damp dungeon. Still, roll on tomorrow. There's some sort of celebration feast planned. At least I think so. The jailer just told me I'm getting the chop. See ya.

HAROLD ROBBINS

15th June

It was a hot, steamy, bright, hazy, baking, boiling, adjective of a day. I stood alone at the roadside, yet not alone, although the shroud of loneliness hung around me like leaves on a tree in autumn. I wondered if I'd ever make it as a big shot writer. In Arizona that day it was 112 degrees in the shade. I was glad I was in California.

A car hurtled lazily towards me down the highway. I stuck out my thumb, it stopped, so did the car. I recognised a familiar, pretty face behind the wheel, it was Charity Ball, movie starlet. I knew it was pretty familiar. She sat there smouldering, lighting a cigarette. She made no sign of protest as I slid across her upholstery. We drove off.

I looked across at Charity, her golden hair, her tanned skin and her firm breasts that strained against her clinging bright orange 70% polyester sweater. I watched her beautiful, slender hands as she changed gear into a stunning blush pink lurex number. She casually mentioned in passing that she was a raging nymphomaniac. Wow, my luck was in, somebody who couldn't help stealing things!

I had nowhere to sleep that night until Charity provocatively whispered she would be pleased to put me up for the night. There would be no problem as her husband was abroad that night. But tomorrow he's probably be dressed as a man.

As soon as we got through the door she tore off all her clothes. Charity certainly did begin at home. She was an animal in bed so I decided it would be more hygienic to sleep on the sofa. That night we made love seven times, it's amazing what you can do with the letters on a scrabble board if you try.

16th June

Charity told me her husband is the big book publisher, Max Clutz, and made an appointment for me to see him. He is a genuine guy with an open mind. I guess that explains the hatchet in his forehead. He gave me a job and I suppose it won't be long until I'm a multi-millionaire treating everybody like a doormat. After all, that is the American way of life.

CLIFF RICHARD

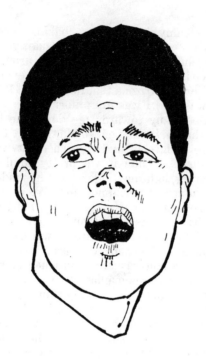

12th. of Never

Trying to plan a summer holiday hot enough to make really strong shadows. Can I find a living doll to go with? I'm still a bachelor boy, so I could go with some other young ones and we'll look for a devil woman. Must remember to carrie my Walkman so I'll be wired for sound. . .

RONALD REAGAN

Tuesday

Stayed in and ironed my neck.

Wednesday

Made love. The earth moved, maybe I'm pressing the wrong button.

ROMMEL

Monday

Ach, ze vezzer is zo hot here in zer dezert, und I am schvetting as zo I haf der hosenpipen unter dem armpitz. Mein uniformen ist covered in zer kleine stains. Und zis ist fery bad for der discipline becoz ze men zink I haf forgotten to shaken ze villy after grosen ger pissenmaken.

Tuesday

Donner und Blitzen, zer vas eine nazi schmell in der bed today und ven I taken down zer panzers, zer ist eine kleine rodent, ja, eine maus, livink in mein vy-fronts. Gott in himmel, zos desert rats are everywhere. Especially since zey hav zer new commander, Montgomery, ze inventor off der hot air balloon. Viz him I shall make der full frontal assault, zen later on maybe ve get married and live in der nice cottage in Norfolk.

Wednesday

Fought ze Battle of der Bulge today. Lost half eine stone.

Thursday

Vent to zee eine Gypsy voman in Cairo. She zaid zat ve vould lose ze three Vorld Vars. 1914–18, 1939–45 und 1966. Gott damn zat Geoff Hurst.

Friday

Heard eine gut yoke at HQ today. Why are ze French roads lined wiz trees? Zo zat ze German army can march in ze shade. Zat von vill have zem rolling in ze Führer bunker.

VIDAL SASSOON

18th February

All day long has it rained, a miserable swirling mist engulfs the world in its sad saturated blanket. But here I stand, fortunate to fight another day, here I stand armed with comb and scissor to ward off the adversary. Before me trudge old ladies, mis-shapen heads distorted with rollers and perming lotion and the room is rife with a stench not unlike mustard gas. My ears jangle with the permanent bombardment of high-speed hairdryers and the ceaseless, pointless chatter and machine gun rattle of loose false teeth. I am not much longer for this world, already gangrene has infected my every finger; my mistake, it's styling gel. As a friend of mine once said to me: 'If I die think only this of me. There is a corner in a foreign land which will always be—Chez Henri.'

SOUSA

Monday

Today I visited my parents, it was good to see oom-Papa and oomMama. When people ask me who had the greatest influence on my music, I have to admit it was my OomPapa, OomPapa, Oompa, Oompa, OomPapa.

CAPTAIN SCOTT

20 Monday	SNOWED !
21 Tuesday	SNOWED !
22 Wednesday	SNOWED !
24 Thursday	SNOWED !
25 Friday	
26 Saturday	SNOWED YESTERDAY !

'I dropped that one two weeks ago—has it only just thawed out?'

SNOW WHITE

Monday

Felt Grumpy all day.

STALIN

MONDAY   HAD A PURGE TODAY!

TUESDAY

PURGED ALL DAY LONG

WEDNESDAY

PURGED!

THURSDAY

DAY OF PURGING

FRIDAY

EVEN PURGED MYSELF TODAY.
MARVELLOUS THINGS THE SENOPODS!

SATURDAY

6.00 PM   SENT FOLLOWING STATEMENT TO
U.S. EMBASSY.
" THE INSIDIOUS NATURE OF IMPERIALIST,
CAPITALIST IDEOLOGY SHALL NO LONGER
BE ALLOWED TO SUBVERT THE HEARTS
AND MINDS OF THE SONS AND DAUGHTERS
INFLUENCES IN THE FIELDS OF ART,
LITERATURE AND TELECOMUNICATIONS SHALL
BE PURGED FROM THE BOWELS OF THE
SOVIET STATE."
8.00 PM   WATCHED DALLAS!

SUPERMAN

Thursday

Learnt to fly today.

Is it a bird? Is it a plane? No, it's Superman.

ALBERT SCHWEITZER

Tuesday

At last, I am now cosily ensconced in the missionary position. But there's so much to do, so many people to help. Mind you, the lepers in the colony are always willing to give a hand. I am having a bit of trouble with the voodoo, so I'll pick up the penicillin tomorrow.

SCHUBERT

November 4th . . .

Started symphony tonight. Finish it tomorrow.

SOLOMON

December 9th . . .

Boy, was I wise today. I was out in the desert and I noticed how the tribes all gathered together in one place to trade. And if there's one thing Arabs like to do, it's shop . . . so I've opened up a big store for them. I call it HERODS. Already they want to buy it.

The Queen of Sheba's coming for dinner tonight. She's a bit upset because in my country everyone is proud of me and calls me wise and everything, but where Sheba comes from all they do is call their dogs after her. Quite appropriate really, but don't say I said so.

I was sitting on the throne today, kinging, when the door burst open and in walked two women and a little baby. It turned out both women claimed the baby as their own and said there must've been some mistake down the hospital. I said, 'So?' They were adamant that each was the mother. Now, I'd been in a similar incident, reversed, when the Queen of Sheba thought she was pregnant last month. I got out of it, 'cos I said, it was me, King David or the Children of Israel. Anyhow, I told these two women that if they both wanted the child I'd get my guard to cut the little bastard in two. He was bawling all over the place anyway. But one mother said, 'No. Let my child live. *She* can have him.' No wonder they call me Solomon the Wise.

Better get ready for Sheba. As that great scribe, Jimmus Tarbuckus, says, 'King Solomon's Mines, the Queen of Sheba's anybody's.'

WILLIAM SHAKESPEARE

29th July 1601

For all my life I have lived in poverty, spending much time and effort producing my plays. But today a greatly fortunate event has occurred and as a result I will be ale to live in luxury for the rest of my life. . Many tradesmen have offered me 'sponsorship' if I will 'advertise' their products in my plays.

I have been able to accommodate many of them, in return for vast sums of money, of course. The tragedy, 'Hamlet', will include scenes of the Prince casually puffing a cheroot and will now be known as 'Hamlet, Prince Panatella of Denmark'. 'A Winter's Tale' will be embroidered with interesting information concerning central heating, while 'The Merchant of Venice' will be particularly useful for those who are considering a bank loan. 'Richard the Third' will be endorsing a medicinal spray that eases those aggravating backaches that you get after a long day's evil-doing, whereas 'Macbeth' will promote a brand new toilet soap that can wash away those stubborn personal stains. Mind you, I have drawn the line at advertising contraceptives in 'Romeo and Juliet', after all, love, it is art.

SATAN

−6 million BC

It makes me want to spit, dear diary, the things people say about me. It's bad enough I get blamed for everything that goes wrong . . . raining on Churchill's funeral . . . Princess Di getting pregnant again . . . but this is the last straw. Someone's only trying to bump that Arthur Scargill off and send him down here. I mean, I'm trying to run the fires of eternal damnation down here, you know . . . it's not for a boy-scouts' sing-song . . . I mean, these are the furnaces of hell, you know, dearie . . . I need my coal. I know what happens . . . they go up to that St Peter, he looks in his book and says: 'You're not down here, sir, go to hell.'

Now, to put the tin helmet on it, I'm shorthanded up on Earth. All these exorcists who've been coming out of the woodwork, cleansing the souls of my disciples. I mean, look at that Rod Stewart. Nearly normal now. I'm going to have to have him repossessed.

I always said that Jesus was dad's favourite.

ISAAC MERRITT SINGER

Monday
Not feeling so good today.

Tuesday
Slightly better.

Wednesday
Sew sew.

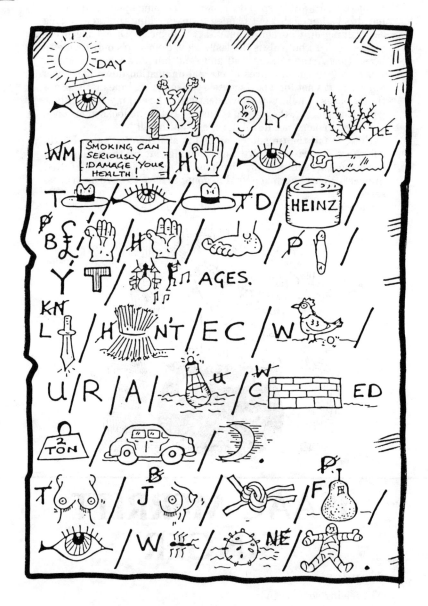

Sunday
I woke up this morning and I saw that I had bean *bound hand and foot in white bandages. Life aint easy when you are a buoy called* Two Ton Car Moon. *It's just* knot *fair, I want my mummy.*

DICK TURPIN

February 4th . . .

Who'd be a highwayman? What a day I've had. It all
started when I went up to Blackheath to stop the
14.20 from Glasgow. It was packed full with screaming
Scottish football fans heading for Wembly. I said,
'Your money or your life.' Three hours later they're
still trying to make up their minds.

Then I stopped the 17.45 from York. There was only
one fat lady on board so I said, 'Stand and deliver.'
How was I to know she was pregnant? That took
another hour and a half just hosing Black Bess down.

Finally I went out to the Great West Road to
ambush the 19.00 from London to Liverpool. At 20.00
it still hadn't arrived but I wasn't unduly concerned
and I was only slightly worried at 21.30. I was plan-
ning what I would do. First I would shoot the driver,
then, after I'd robbed the passengers, I would garotte
the male passengers, then rape and finally strangle
the women. After that I'd eat the horses. At 23.45 I
was getting worried. I hope nothing's happened to
them. Then I remembered. The Great West Road's
one way now. Went home.

'No, no!—I said stand and deliver!'

MARK THATCHER

May 19th . . .

Ah, there you are, diary, bet you thought I'd got lost.

October 21st . . .

Ah, there you are, diary, bet you thought I'd got lost. It was my first day at the new school today. Gosh, I like it but it took me five and a half hours to get home tonight. Then Daddy told me it was a boarding school. Mum said I should take a bath and go to bed . . . so that was another hour and a half hunting for the spanners before Daddy told me Mummy meant *have* a bath. Gosh, it's jolly exciting, anyway, just being the son of the Prime Minister. By golly, my mum's subjects don't much like her, you know . . . they say she's responsible for everyone not having a job . . . and I must say Daddy and I agree with them. That nice Mr Kinnock says my Mummy's intransigent . . . so I'm going there to visit her.

Next April 23rd . . .

Ah, there you are, diary, bet you thought I'd got lost.

TARZAN

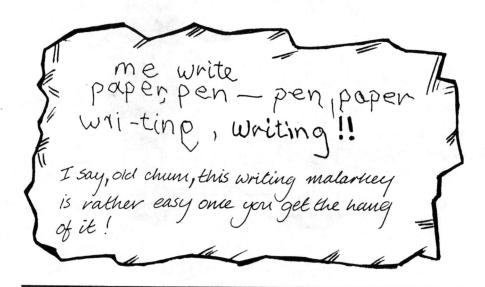

ELIZABETH TAYLOR

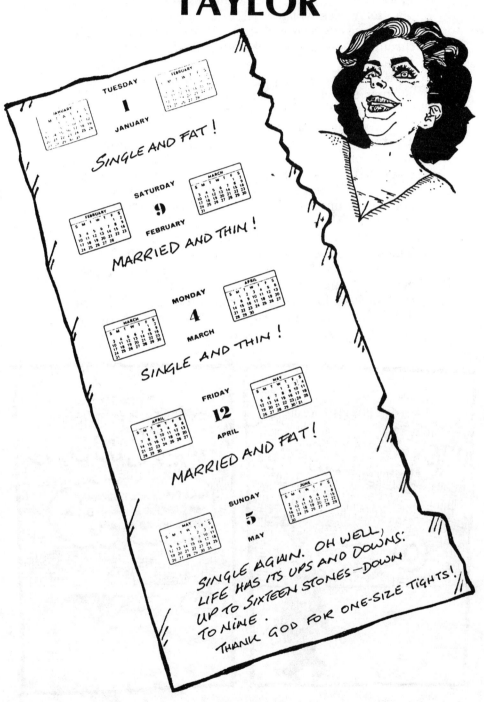

TUESDAY
1
JANUARY

Single and fat!

SATURDAY
9
FEBRUARY

Married and thin!

MONDAY
4
MARCH

Single and thin!

FRIDAY
12
APRIL

Married and fat!

SUNDAY
5
MAY

Single again. Oh well, life has its ups and downs. Up to sixteen stones — down to nine. Thank God for one-size tights!

DYLAN THOMAS

Since arriving in America I am considering writing a play for voices which I will call, 'Under Hollywood'.

Only we can hear and see their dreams as they glide through their lumbering slumber, their scanty fantasies of fame and fortune, their perpetual paralytic parties in that rich, pitch, black dark. The constant sucking up, chit-chat, backslap, backstab and bold-faced lies of the petty, petit-fours partiers.

Wandering through this well-fed carnival of crystal-clinking carnivores, we plumb the depths and heights of the winners and losers. Budding starlets, stage-struck and stunning, study proceedings with an ambitious eagle eye. While stealthy wealthy producers loosely encircle the girl to nurture her like a vulture under their limb-cracking wings.

In the wings stand the old ones, the forgotten famous faces whose features fade like heated wax. They chase the face they used to have, they prompted many a romantic fantasy. But now gone forever, taken to be melted down so another may take its place in the dream factory. Under Hollywood, where they dream of living, where living is a dream.

J.R. TOLKIEN

Today, I left on a quest, a journey of great importance that would take me to many strange places in many strange lands. My task was to find the king. I set off and was given directions by the black horse, the stag, the swan, the red dragon and the dog and fox. That night I stopped at the castle but he wasn't there and then went in search of the blacksmith with guidance from the seven stars. Finally, I arrived exhausted and collapsed into the king's arms. I was pissed as a newt, now that's what I call a pubcrawl.

TOULOUSE-LAUTREC

Monday

Had part in a Western movie. Played a low-down bum.

'I think Toulouse is getting a complex about his height.'

U UNDERWOOD

September 3rd . . .

Ah yes, this is creativity, diary, this is what book writing is all about. You cannot imagine the swell of pride, the orgasm of delight, the sheer joy produced by my enthusiastic heart when my creative adrenalin is flowing out of control and forming rapids over the rocks of tedium latterly in my brain. The opening line to my new novel etched its way into my sleepy brain seconds ago and is responsible for my good cheer. This opening line, of a quality the world has not seen before, will, I promise you, be the most read, most talked about, most analysed opening line of any novel, before or yet to be. It has style, pace, wit, life, it is memorable yet forgettable, it is poignant yet dull. I am going to set it down on this page today, diary, because this is the day of its birth.

I seem to have forgotten it.

tHequick Bron FOcx JUmpEd ov er the LAZt dog.
You'll read that line a few times in your life.

Dad says I should work at my typing machine just in case the book doesn't work out.

V GUISEPPE VERDI

Peple-a dey aska me, hey Guiseppe, why you no writa da music no more? An I say, why I wanna writa da musik when I gotta da nice-a pizza place in-a Pimlico? Oh, sure, ess-a very nice for to make-a music. But as-a mamma used to say, Aïda and Othello ainta gonna sell no spaghetti! Anyway, I ainta called Guiseppe Verdi no more! Is-a just plain Joe Green.

PANCHO VILLA

Tuesday

I hate the government, I hate the bureaucrats, I hate the rich and I'm not too keen about being named after a holiday home in Majorca.

VENUS DE MILO

Sat

Bad news about the statue . . . the sculptor can't do arms.

'It's for art, luv!'

QUEEN VICTORIA

1872.

Unveiled Albert's memorial in the park today . . . case comes up next week.

VON TRAPP FAMILY

22nd September 1939

I needed some dough, a deer, a female deer, so I went to see Ray, a drop of golden sun, in the hope that he might lend some money to me, a name I call myself. He said this time I'd gone too far, a long long way to run. So, a needle pulling thread, what? I'd go back to LA, a note to follow so and be back there in time for tea, a drink with jam and bread. But how could I do that if I didn't have any money? Which brings us back to dough, dough, dough, dough.

VAN GOGH

June 3rd . . .

Went crazy and chopped ear off. Now it looks as if I'll have to give up painting. Hat keeps falling over my eyes.

'Well, doc, I was cutting off my ear for my loved one when the knife slipped.'

JULES VERNE

July 17th . . .

Been extremely busy all day working on new books about unusual journeys fraught with danger and undertaken in strange crafts. And when I *finish* the new bus timetable, I'll get on with one of my novels.

I've got this idea about how there's another civilisation underwater. They have countries and cities and people same as us but they don't have wars. Instead all the inhabitants of this other world fight all their battles on the football ground. I call it 'Twenty Thousand Leagues under the sea'.

Not getting on too well with my current book all about this bet where my hero is meant to go around the world in eighty days. I'm at Chapter 16 and he's still stuck in the contraflow on the M1. Serves me right for letting him eat at the Granada near Junction 8.

Still, at least my latest published work is selling well. The one about all the people who need work go to this big organisation in London and get help. It's called 'GLC', or 'Journey to the Job Centre of the Earth'.

ST VITUS

Friday

Went to the dance tonight. Had fit and won second prize.

WILBUR WRIGHT

December 17th . . .

What a sensation! Flying through the air like a bird. It was all I'd hoped it would be. Exhilaratingly dangerous. I loved it. My brother Orville was like a big kid. First of all he was so air sick he used my paper bag as well. He was so scared I had to drag him to the tarmac and push him on. He was shaking and blubbering all over the place. It was so bad at one point I even considered piloting the thing myself. But eventually I got him settled . . . by letting him have his parachute open . . . We were flying over Kitty Hawk when I had my great vision that perhaps there was a money-making business in these flying machines. Wilbur had accidentally looped the loop . . . I'd given him some barley sugar for his ears and one of the lumps had fallen out . . . and in his efforts to retrieve this the plane had done a somersault. All that happened was my lunch box fell out and that's what gave me my idea for a great airline . . . Lost luggage. People would keep coming back forever . . . unless they found their suitcase.

'Wilbur, I don't know if you'll get that thing off the ground.'

RIP VAN WINKLE

1803–1843.

Slept in.

WELLINGTON

April 5th . . .

It is 1815 and I go to meet the little Frenchman at Waterloo
. . . why Charles Aznavour couldn't come in to Heathrow
like everyone else I'll never know. I called my batman over
and he said: 'The new footwear for the battle, Duke?' I said:
'No, it could be messy . . . chuck over my old boots.'

H.G. WELLS

Monday

At last my time machine is ready. This afternoon I will find
out if it actually works!

Sunday

I have spent all day building my time machine and making
the delicate final adjustments.

Saturday

I woke up this morning with the most improbable idea, a
machine that can take a man back in time. I will draw up the
plans today and start the construction tomorrow.

THE THREE WISE MEN

December 25th

We followed a star. Just love that Barry Manilow.

'I think you'll find the list says frankincense*!'*

BARNES WALLACE

Have thought of a great idea—the Bouncing Bomb. The idea came to me at half past twelve last night when I was with Elsie, the barmaid, on her waterbed.

JOHN WAYNE

Quite a day! I got the girl who wore the yellow ribbon, with true grit I won a couple of gunfights, sailed the seven seas, sank the entire Japanese fleet, settled the Korean question and was pretty damn useful in Vietnam. Went home and did the hoovering.

DR WATSON

8th July, 9 am

As I awoke this morning in our apartment in Baker Street I was immediately aware of a strange acrid aroma which seemed to hang like a cloud filling the entire room. As my senses slowly came to me, I realised that it was Sherlock Holmes smugly sucking on a churchwarden's pipe.

'I thought you said it was all over between you and the church-warden, Holmes?' I said.

'Quite right, Watson,' replied Holmes smugly. 'It is all over, but you need not worry, for I myself shall do the cleaning up today.'

'Oh really, Holmes,' I said in disgust, 'how utterly tasteless.'

The rubber sheet squeaked slightly as the churchwarden rolled on to the damp patch. I got out of bed.

The bright December mornings were bitingly cold, so I was glad that it was July. As I stood at the window listening I heard the sound of a wild cat being slowly castrated with a blunt chain saw. 'I say, Holmes,' I said, 'would you mind not playing your violin, I have a headache?'

'I know you have, Watson,' he replied smugly, 'in fact I know everything about you. I bet I know exactly what your next word will be.'

'What?' I asked.

'Precisely,' said Holmes smugly, sticking the syringe into his arm with a smug grin.

1 pm

The sun winked intermittently between the clouds as the car crept insidiously, just like Nicholas Parsons, through the country lanes. We had just passed through the villages of Much Drinkwater and Large Piddle-on-the-Looe. The green fields put me in mind of the hallowed places of my youth in the town of Red Ink Under Line. I remembered how I used to cycle past lake Windermere to help mother with the weekly shopping. Sometimes Winderfriends.

'I say, Holmes,' I said, waking from my reverie, 'do you know who the murderer is?'

'Of course,' he said smugly, 'I know everything.'

'How did you become so brilliant, Holmes? Was it your school? Which school did you attend?'

'Elementary, my dear Watson,' he said smugly.

From the window I saw the neat perimeter fences of the Hill-man Hunter estate. The car pulled into the drive and slowed to a halt outside the impressive mansion house. We got out of the car and I looked at the plaque on the wall, while Holmes looked at the plaque on my teeth. It said 'Superior Manor. No Hawkers. No Siddeleys. Tradesman and perverts please use rear entrance.' Holmes rang the bell. The door opened and there, framed in the doorway, was a wrinkled old retainer.

'Good day, gentlemen', he said, 'I am Scrote, the butler.'

'What?' I said.

'No sir, Watt is the chauffeur.'

'Watt is the chauffeur?' said Holmes.

'The chauffeur is the man who drives the car, sir,' replied the butler. He showed us into the study. 'His lordship will join you soon, gentlemen.'

The door opened. His lordship entered the room. He was smoking a large King Edward. Why he had a potato in his mouth was behond even Holmes's powers of deduction. His lordship was a tall boy with long sideboards and a large chest. He had made a lot of money in the furniture business.

'Ah, Mr Holmes and Dr Watson,' he said. 'Delighted to meet you. Especially you, Holmes. I was at school with your brother, Barratt Holmes, in fact we were in the same house together. How is the old wreck?'

'No time for pleasantries, you bastard,' said Holmes smugly. 'I know who the killer is.'

'Oh really?' said his lordship casually.

'Yes. My lord, you are the killer,' said Holmes smugly.

'Oh really? I always thought cancer was the killer,' said his lordship smugly.

'Don't say things smugly,' said Holmes, 'I'm the smug one around here. And I warn you, don't reach casually into the inside pocket of your smoking jacket.'

His lordship reached, casually, into the inside pocket of his smoking jacket. With the speed of a cat Holmes took out his Mauser and shot his lordship three times. Meow, meow, meow. His lordship collapsed in a pile on the floor.

'Did you do that pile, Watson?' asked Holmes smugly.

'Sorry, Holmes,' I said sheepishly.

Slowly, I walked to the body lying on the floor and removed his lordship's smoking jacket. 'No time for that now, Watson,' said Holmes smugly. As I removed his lordship's hand, to my horror I saw that there was no gun, only a solid silver cigarette case engraved with his lordship's initials, H.L.

'So,' said Holmes smugly, 'the warning was correct. Cigarettes *can* seriously damage your health.'

7 pm

The evening sun, like a 75-year-old sex maniac, was fast losing its power as its day gradually drifted to a close. Holmes sat in the corner of the apartment, an opium-induced smile playing smugly on his lips.

'Well, Holmes,' I ventured, 'another case solved and another villain brought to justice. I don't know how you do it, Holmes. I really don't. I say, Holmes, I know I'm a little stupid sometimes.'

'Oh Watson, you underestimate yourself,' said Holmes, 'occasionally you can be extremely stupid.'

'Quite so, Holmes, quite so. But if you don't mind my asking, there is just one part of the story that has been puzzling me all day and try as I might I just can't seem to work it out.'

'Yes, Watson?'

'Well, what happened to the churchwarden?'

MAE WEST

So the navy has a new life jacket which when inflated reminds them of me, so they've called it the Mae West. You fall in the water with one of these on and you float until they find you. Now they're working on the Dolly Parton where you don't even get wet.

WAGNER

Thursday

Finished ring cycle today. Working on handlebars tomorrow.

MUDDY WATERS

Didn't wake up this morning.

WILLIAM WORDSWORTH

11th September

I have been moved deeply by the sight of the most beautiful flower I have ever seen, so I wrote a poem.

I hung about all on me tod,
Waiting like a stupid sod,
Looking at nature and that kind of stuff,
I passed the time picking navel fluff.

Then blimey O'Riley, cop an eyeful of these,
A bunch of daffs a-fluttering on the breeze,
I thought they was daffs, they were yellow and that,
When a bloke called 'em tulips, I did feel a pratt.

X XERXES

Janus maximus

Got beaten at Thermopylae . . . even though I had a hotel on Mayfair.

XAVIERA HOLLANDER

June 19th . . . pm.

Went to the doctor. He said if I stay on my feet for a few days he'll have me back in bed in no time.

June 20th . . . pm.

Great night. Made thirty dollars. Now I wish I'd charged them twenty cents each.

June 21st . . . pm.

Had a check up. Funny, I didn't notice him in the queue.

Y DUKE OF YORK

Had ten thousand men . . . case comes up next week. I got caught when they were only halfway up.

Z ZEPPELIN

October 15th . . .

Very much troubled by an onslaught of wind. Went to the doctor and he gave me something for it. A balloon. I filled it up in an hour. But it gave me a great idea. Suppose I got a giant balloon that could actually carry people. I could fill the seating capacity with all the flatulent people from my doctor's waiting-room and we could use their natural processes as a sort of fuel. Fly my balloon out over the oceans from continent to continent with the semi-incontinent. And if the balloon won't fly and comes down with all those on board perishing . . . who'd give a monkey's?

The wife said last night that I went down like a lead zeppelin.

ZORBA

March 23rd

Boy, did I have a skinful last night. I drank twenty five bottles of ouzo. Some people round here call me Absorber the Greek now. A nasty rumour has sprung up that Greek men are not fussy about the sex of their partners when they make love. This is a filthy rumour put about by greedy male tourists who fall for the old five drachma piece on the pavement trick. Of course my new dance is meant to imply by its rhythm the act of lovemaking . . . slow at first . . . gentle . . . then frantic. I should talk about fussy . . . you should see my wife. Now you know why I dance sideways.

ZORRO

Friday

I'm sick of it, I'm just too polite. I always end up at the back of the queue, at the cimena, at the supermarket, at the fish and chip shop. And if anybody ever writes about me, I end up being sodding last again! See what I mean.